THE ORIGINS OF THE CRISIS BETWEEN ISRAEL AND THE PALESTINIANS

THE **ORIGINS** OF THE **CRISIS BETWEEN** ISRAEL AND THE PALESTINIANS

ITS CAUSES AND HOW TO ADDRESS THEM

ISMAIL RIFAAT

THE ORIGINS OF THE CRISIS BETWEEN ISRAEL AND THE PALESTINIANS
Its Causes and How to Address Them

iUniverse books may be ordered through booksellers or by contacting:

iUniverse
1663 Liberty Drive
Bloomington, IN 47403
www.iuniverse.com
844-349-9409

ISBN: 978-1-4917-6829-7 (sc)
ISBN: 978-1-4917-6828-0 (e)

Library of Congress Control Number: 2015909252

Print information available on the last page.

iUniverse rev. date: 01/17/2024

Contents

Preface

The most topical issues being discussed worldwide today relate to ominous developments in the Middle East (ME), and to international efforts to contain their menacing threats.

Current conditions in several Moslem countries in the region reflect a dire state of affairs. The manifestations of problems are painfully evident. They include lack of security, civil wars, the death, injury and uprooting of millions of innocent people, and the collapse or ineffectiveness of several national governments. In particular, action by radical Islamist entities such as the Islamic State for Iraq and Syria (ISIS; also referred to as ISIL), is threatening the security of both Middle Eastern and Western countries. Furthermore, the pace of deterioration of conditions in some ME countries such as Iraq, Syria, Libya, and Yemen could accelerate with potentially more ominous consequences.

The book aims to address these conditions by exploring the historical developments that contributed to the emergence of this sad state of affairs, and proposes ways to address identified problems.

Writing the book was inspired by the events that took place on June 30th, and July 3rd of 2013 in Egypt, whereby elected President Morsi was ousted from power. I felt that this development was extremely significant. On July 12, 2013 I posted an article on my website. It partially states:

"Here in the US we have just celebrated the fourth of July. The French will soon celebrate the fourteenth of July.

I feel that the third of July -the day the Egyptian army ousted former President Morsi- might assume a similar status in the annals of history. … the army -presumably- acted in response to overwhelming popular outrage. It is specifically the nature of the outrage, rather than the army's action, that is most significant in considering the third of July as a potentially historic date. From what I have seen and heard, *the outrage seems to reflect a sentiment that craves emancipation from religious radicalism; as such it could usher a new era of rational and sustainable development, both in Egypt and elsewhere.*"

Debate was raging at the time -and continues today- about a breach of democracy and a military coup d'état in Egypt. The US particularly expressed concerns in this respect. However, while quite appreciative of these concerns, I was sympathetic with the revolution, and started writing in its defense and support.

My sympathy with the revolution of July 2013 related primarily to its success in reversing the tide of growing Islamist movements in the Middle East. For decades I observed how radical Islamism was growing, and was deeply concerned about this trend. The momentous developments involving warring radical Islamists in Iraq, Syria, Libya, and Yemen which erupted in late 2014 vindicated my fears, and prompted me to continue writing to complete this book.

I am an Egyptian born US citizen, an architect/Planner with substantial international experience in these fields. I did not receive any formal education in political science or other disciplines traditionally related to the subject matter of the book. Also, I have not been directly involved in politics neither in Egypt nor here in the USA. This being the case, I wish to clarify at the outset how I feel confident about addressing conditions in the Middle East.

I come from a middle class Egyptian family. Similar families often sent their kids to private schools; usually, girls to French schools, and boys to English schools. My father elected to send me and my two brothers to public schools. He said: if you are to live in Egypt, you have to share the experience and education of the majority of the young people of the country. As it turned out, I left Egypt in Januray1959 shortly after graduating from the University of Alexandria on a post-graduate scholarship to Switzerland, and never returned to live in Egypt since then. Sadly, as I will recount, conditions in Egypt changed in certain ways that precluded my return to pursue a promising career.

I lived in Switzerland for over eight years and in Canada for a couple of years before immigrating to the USA in mid 1967. Later on, I worked and lived intermittently in Kuwait, Qatar, Dubai, and Saudi Arabia. Over the years, I returned to Egypt occasionally on professional assignments and as a tourist.

The fact that I went to public schools and to University in Egypt confirms my intimate knowledge of Egyptian society. The kind of people-sense that one develops from growing up with other young people and feeling the impact of developments jointly with others cannot be matched. As I grew up in Egypt, I experienced firsthand certain developments that are particularly relevant to the evolution of the current crisis.

Egypt is a prominent country in the ME region, and developments there have had, and are likely to continue to have far reaching consequences in the region. Also, the USA -especially after the demise of the British Empire- exerted profound influence on developments in the ME, and is likely to continue to be actively involved in the affairs of the region. Over the years, I had a keen interest in following up on developments both in Egypt and the Middle East, as well as related developments here in the USA. This provided me with insights that are pertinent to the subject matter of the book.

Thus, my relevant international experience, and my continued interest in developments in the Middle East primed me to write this book.

The book is not conceived as an academic discourse where statements are buttressed by foot notes and references. Certain data, such as the accepted spelling of Arabic names, and the description and dates of certain relevant events were sometimes obtained on line. Irrespective however, I wish to assert that citing the sources of information, has little to do with the thrust of my arguments which are intended to focus on the issues that I have identified from personal experience. Thus, the book is essentially an expression of my own impressions, and views, and reflects how I feel and think about the problems of the Middle East.

As I present my assessments with due humility however, I wish to point out that few 'experts' in ME affairs have the kind of experience and intimate understanding of historical developments as I do.

Introduction

Southwest Asia / North Africa

Map of the Middle East, Courtesy NASA Outline Maps
Names of countries added by the author; Gaza and the occupied Palestinian
territories are not highlighted due to the small scale of the map.

Several definitions of the Term "Middle East" exist and are in
use by different international entities. The un-shaded areas in the
above map depict NASA's version. For the purposes of this book,
I add Pakistan and North Sudan to the definition of "Middle
East"; they are often included by others.

The book is not intended to cover developments in each country
in the region in a comprehensive manner; rather, it focuses on

addressing issues relevant to the current crisis. Also, critical issues are covered only by citing relevant examples.

The populations of all the countries of the ME region as depicted above are predominantly Moslem, with one exception, namely, Israel which has a majority of Jewish citizens and which proclaims itself as a Jewish State. The populations of the Moslem countries of the ME are generally recognized as Arabs, with the exception of Turkey, Iran, Afghanistan, and Pakistan. Egypt and Israel lie at the geographic center of gravity of the region.

As I mentioned, developments in Egypt have and will continue to influence developments in the ME, and I happen to be intimately familiar with the evolution of conditions in Egypt. Thus, chapter 1 recounts pertinent personal experience as I grew up and as I occasionally visited the country after my departure in 1959. This and other observations from abroad reveal the evolution and the underlying causes of certain relevant problems in Egypt, which happen to mirror conditions in the region at large. Commonly, issues relate to the creation and subsequent action of the State of Israel, to interventions by Western Powers, and to the attitudes and action of Moslem populations and their political and religious leaders.

Having identified the roots of problems one could contemplate potential approaches to address the current crisis. Thus, chapters 2, 3, and 4 are concerned with addressing the three underlying roots of problems indicated above. I express my views in their respect, and suggest potential action to deal with each of the identified issues.

As the title of the book implies, Islamism is a glaring symptom of the current crisis. I use "Islamism" to refer to a slew of ideologies which I consider to deviate from the spirit of Islam. Some forms of Islamism are perhaps comparable to Zionism. Some lethal forms of extreme deviant Islamism have recently emerged though, and are evident in the current crisis. Thus, Islamism is reflected in many forms ranging from the kind displayed by the Moslem Brotherhood (MB) movement which originated in Egypt, to that displayed by the notorious ISIS in Iraq and Syria. By my definition, Islamism is reflected in the actions of "Islamists".

Analysis clearly indicates that Zionist action contributed to the emergence of Islamist movements in the ME. Therefore, chapter 5 addresses the Ideologies of Zionism and Islamism and the consequences of their involvement in state affairs.

An Epilogue sums up deliberations.

Chapter 1

A PERSONAL PERSPECTIVE OF PERTINENT DEVELOPMENTS IN EGYPT

Since the days of the pharos, Egypt existed as a coherent society for millennia. It is distinctive in this respect. Due to its central location and to its significance in the ancient civilized world which continued over many centuries, it attracted the interest of, and was invaded and occupied by the Greek, Roman, Islamic Caliphates, French, Ottoman, and British Empires.

Egypt's modern history starts with Mohammed Ali who established the rule of his dynasty in 1805. During his reign Egypt reemerged as a global power. He built a naval fleet that threatened the imperial powers of the day to the point that they conspired to sink it in the battle of Navarino in 1827; one of my great-great grandfathers was sent by Mohammed Ali to study ship building in France, and was instrumental in building the Egyptian armada in Alexandria.

I learned from the elders of my family that Egypt experienced a renaissance during the 19th century which lasted into the early 20th century. The country had a strong economy derived from the export of commodities such as cotton. The Egyptian pound around the nineteen hundreds was worth more than five Pounds Sterling. At some point it was worth more than 30 Swiss Francs. Today, one Swiss Franc is worth more than 12 Egyptian pounds; i.e. the

Egyptian pound is now worth about 1% of what it used to be worth in terms of Western currencies during the Egyptian renaissance.

Egypt was prosperous to an extent that attracted Europeans of different nationalities to settle in the country. For example, many Greeks and Cypriots lived in Egypt. They owned high end restaurants, confectionaries, and grocery stores; I frequented many as I grew up in Alexandria.

Mohammed Ali and his descendants were intent on building a modern infrastructure; Egypt had a functional railroad system in the eighteen fifties ahead of most countries in the world. They relied on borrowing funds from Western Powers to implement their ambitious programs. In particular, Khedive Ismail who commissioned the construction of the Suez Canal brought the country to the brink of bankruptcy. Various developments, including fear that Egypt will default on repayment of its loans to Western Powers gave the British an excuse to invade and occupy Egypt in 1882. They continued to occupy Egypt for 70 years until 1952.

Before the British occupation, my father's grandfather on his mother's side, Ismail Sabry, gained a scholarship to study law in Paris, France; I was named after him. He became attorney general of Egypt, Deputy Minister of Justice, and Governor of Alexandria. He was also a prominent poet, and earned the title 'Pasha'; "Beik" and "Pasha" were titles like "Sir", and "Lord" conveyed by the rulers upon those who deserved recognition for distinctive service. My father told me that, after the British occupation, Ismail Sabry was approached by someone high up in the British Commission in Egypt to become minister or prime minister -I do not recall exactly- on 'certain conditions'. My father told me anecdotally that Ismail Sabry chased the British official out of his office.

The last ruling descendant of Mohammed Ali, King Farouk, assumed power after the death of his father King Fouad on April 28, 1936; the day I was born in Cairo.

My father Ibrahim Rifaat graduated as a civil engineer from Fouad University -now Cairo University- and received a scholarship to study at the Federal Institute of Technology (FIT) in Zurich where he obtained another Diploma and a Doctorate in civil/structural engineering. He went to Zurich in the late nineteen twenties, and returned to Egypt in the early nineteen thirties. My father and his Egyptian colleagues were recognized for their scholastic excellence at the FIT. Confirming Egypt's affluence at the time, they used to muse about how well they lived in Switzerland, solely on the stipend that they received from the Egyptian Government.

Shortly upon his return to Egypt, my father was appointed professor at the newly founded Farouk University -now the University of Alexandria- and became one of the founders of the Faculty of Engineering there. He later founded and presided over the Alexandria Chapter of the Society of Professional Engineers. We moved to Alexandria in 1942 where I attended the last year of kindergarten, and later primary and secondary school, and University.

My father was a popular professor, humanist, and progressive thinker of the first order. He received the title Beik for his achievements. I vividly recall him reading from a thick German book about Greek mythology, translating to me and my brothers into Arabic and rhetorically preaching courageous action, bravery, and heroism.

World War II erupted in 1939. Some of my first memories in life relate to the air raids by the Germans and Italians on Alexandria around 1943; I was seven years old then. I can vividly recall the sound of air raid sirens, bomb explosions, and anti aircraft guns blasting. I also recall pulling my reluctant dad's hands out of bed to take shelter in the basement of the apartment building where we lived, and finally, the relief of hearing the safety sirens.

During my boyhood, Egypt continued to be a Constitutional Monarchy. Several political parties were well established, and elections were held regularly to select members of parliament and to establish the majority party that would assume the reins of government. Generally, conditions were similar to other representative democracies, both old and contemporary; a fact that is almost never mentioned or acknowledged in contemporary discourse about Egypt and the ME!!

King Farouk was considered by some to be a womanizing playboy whose excesses were not appreciated. He sometimes consorted with shady and corrupt characters whose actions were deplored. Others claim that he was a patriotic Monarch who cared for his people, but that his efforts were frustrated by the British. The country had a feudal few who owned thousands of acres of land and used those who farmed the land to amass enormous fortunes; some were benevolent while others were not, in a way similar to the founding fathers of the USA who owned and used slaves to farm their lands.

Talking about money in politics, I recall an amusing anecdote about election campaigns in Egypt. It is expressed in Southern Egyptian dialect, calling for the election of a certain candidate. It sounds like this: "Dalal Hussein, radel dadd, yeheb el dadd, we yehott el deneih fi el yadd". Correction of the Southern accent and translation into English, which alas does not rime as well: Galal Hussein is a serious and solid man who puts a pound -then worth many dollars- in your hand.

Of course, as in the USA and elsewhere, the wealthy and powerful exerted substantial and sometimes deleterious influence on political developments. On the positive side though, political and community leaders were on the whole patriotic and ethical individuals. The judiciary was largely independent. My grandfather Hassan Beik Rifaat was Chief Justice of the High Appellate Court in Cairo. I remember sitting next to him in the veranda of his villa in Giza as a young boy, as he reminisced about some of the cases that he judged, and gently lectured me on the virtues of ethical behavior.

Egypt's history since Mohammed Ali clearly reflects secular conditions. Moslems, Copts - Egyptian Orthodox Christians- and Jews generally lived together in peace; albeit, relatively insignificant incidents flared up occasionally between Moslems and Copts. Jewish Egyptians did well financially and were successful in business; for example most department stores were owned by Jews. Secularity prevailed for years even after the 1952 revolution. The following account attests to that.

My family on my father's side loved classical music. My grandmother, my father, my uncle, and three aunts either played a musical instrument or sang. One of my aunts studied at the Cairo Conservatory and composed serious music, and many of my cousins are accomplished pianists. Continuing in the family tradition, my father retained Madam Severi Goldstein to give his sons piano lessons. What piece I played, and how I performed in her student's concert is beside the point, but evokes fond memories. Certain other events relating to the family's love of music are more relevant.

As a young boy, my father used to be invited by his grandfather Ismail Sabry to sit at his literary salon where the most prominent Egyptian poets recited their work; namely, Hafez Ibrahim, Ahmed Shawqi, and Ismail Sabry himself. As a result, my father had a flair for poetry. Later on in his life he developed a hobby combining both his love of music and poetry. He put Arabic words to three operas: La Traviata, Carmen, and Aida. La Traviata was performed to his Arabic words at the Cairo Opera House after I left Egypt. What I experienced firsthand though were the musical evenings at home in Alexandria where his work was rehearsed. Madam Goldstein played the piano, a young Egyptian soprano sang the role of Violetta, and Mr. Goldstein, a tenor, sang the role of

5

Alferdo; he did that in Arabic with a heavy Eastern Block Jewish accent!

Many Jewish Families recall sentimental memories of Egypt reflecting fond recollections that are similar to my own.

Sadly, certain developments impacted and altered conditions in Egypt from economic prosperity and a secular atmosphere of peaceful religious coexistence, to poor economic conditions and an environment promoting religious radicalism, intolerance, and strife.

After WW II ended in 1945, many of the Jewish survivors of the Holocaust committed by the Nazi regime, as well as Russian Jews who were abused by Stalin, had a strong desire to create a state of their own to which they could immigrate, and thus avoid potential future abuses. Their quest is certainly understandable in view of the conditions they had been subjected to. Certain historical developments provided a framework for their subsequent action, namely: the conception of 'Zionism', and an act by the British Empire.

"Zionism" was coined by Nathan Birnbaum in 1890 to signify 'the return of the Jewish people to their homeland to resume Jewish sovereignty over the land of Israel'; the Biblical Judea and Samaria where Moslem, Christian, and Jewish Palestinians were living at the time. It is to be noted that many Jewish religious scholars do not agree with the concept of Zionism and try to distance themselves from its tenets. They point out that the Torah, while defining 'the land of Israel', does not urge the Jews 'to resume Jewish sovereignty over the land of Israel' on their own, rather, the Torah ties the return of the Jews to the advent of the "Messiah", he, is the one who would usher their return. Notwithstanding, Many Jews adopted the notion of Zionism and embarked on an exodus to Palestine.

An act by Great Britain paved the way for the fulfillment of Zionist aspirations, namely, the statement in 1917 known as the Balfour Declaration. A letter from Balfour -then Foreign Minister- to Baron Rothschild, "for transmission to the Zionist Federation of Great Britain and Ireland" stated: "His Majesty's government view with favour the establishment in Palestine of a national home for the Jewish people, and will use their best endeavours to facilitate the achievement of this object, it being clearly understood that nothing shall be done which may prejudice the civil and religious rights of existing non-Jewish communities in Palestine, or the rights and political status enjoyed by Jews in any other country."*

Britain had a mandate from the League of Nations to administer Palestine and Transjordan which it exercised form 1920 to 1948. Conflicts between indigenous Arabs and Jews raged during the British Mandate. Being still in control after WW II, the British initially contained the flow of Jewish immigrants into Palestine within limits prescribed by prevailing international accords. Zionists rejected the restrictions and mounted a campaign of terrorist attacks in an effort to get the British to abandon the restrictions. The Irgun and the Haganah -recognized as terrorist organizations by the New York Times- mounted several assaults to this end; famous among those was the bombing of the King David Hotel in Jerusalem which led to over 90 people of different nationalities killed, and over 45 injured.

Neighboring Arab countries including Egypt, Jordan, and Syria who observed these developments with concern, went to war against the Zionist militias in support of the Palestinians in1948. The Arab forces did not succeed in stemming the tide of Zionist militias, and a cease fire agreement was established in 1949. The agreement entailed the partition of Mandatory Palestine, into Israel, the West Bank under the Jordanian Kingdom, and the All Palestine Government in the Gaza Strip under Egyptian military occupation.

---

* Encyclopedia Britannica / The Balfour Declaration

My father's initial reaction to the Jewish exodus to Palestine was that: many of the European Jewish immigrants are scientists and technologically advanced people. We could embrace them and work together towards a better future for all. However, he had relatives and friends in the army, officers who actually fought the 1948 war; I listened to their accounts of the war when they visited us in Alexandria. Learning about the carnage of the indigenous Palestinian people my father reneged on his position. He was never prejudiced against the Jewish people, and continued to be unbiased towards all religions. He simply did not tolerate the atrocities committed by Zionist militias that were recounted to him by those he trusted.

The war of 1948 ushered an era of conflicts between Israel, and Egypt and other Arab countries, and initiated a process of polarization among Jews and Moslems in general. Lethal conflicts usually impact the general populations of warring entities in certain ways. For example, after Pearl Harbor, Japanese immigrants in the US were derided and prosecuted for no fault of their own. Although not condoned, this seems to be a social phenomenon which lumps certain 'others' as 'our enemy'. In this way, similar sentiments started to emerge in Egypt regarding Egyptian Jews. These sentiments did not lead to far reaching consequences for quite some time.

The years went by, and by 1951 as I was about to graduate from secondary school, riots erupted in opposition to the King and government; I was 15 years old at the time. Schools were closed for a couple of months. I used to systematically attend my classes and do my home work. This usually was enough for me to pass exams with good grades and to move up at school. However, in the lack of instruction for two crucial months at the end of the school year, and the difficulty of securing private tutors due to the great demand for teachers, I failed one subject for the first time in my life; chemistry. I retook the exam and passed on the second round, and thus qualified to go to university.

On July 23, 1952, a group of army officers led by General Muhammad Naguib overthrew King Farouk. Shortly thereafter the military abolished the Constitutional Monarchy and established a new republic, and Naguib became its first president on June 18, 1953. Another leading officer of the revolution, Gamal Abdel Nasser, became Deputy Prime Minister. Nasser forced Naguib out of office and assumed power as President in 1956. He continued to be president until his death in September 1970.

Apart from general dissatisfaction with the Monarchy that I alluded to above, the coup was triggered by the military's disdain of what transpired in the war of 1948 in Palestine. Some complained that corrupt individuals with ties to the Palace, were responsible for providing the army with faulty ammunition and weapons that backfired in the face of soldiers. More importantly, the military being humiliated by defeat did not approve of how the government handled the whole affair from the initiation of the war to what transpired thereafter leading Israel to consolidate its gains and emerge as a sovereign state. Thus, one could link the 1952 military revolution in Egypt and its consequences with the creation of the State of Israel.

My father, not approving of many conditions under King Farouk's reign was sympathetic with the 1952 revolution. He recruited members of the faculty of engineering in Alexandria to join 'Hayaat Al-Tahreer' -the liberation organization- established by the Revolutionary Military Council, and headed one of the local branches of the organization in Alexandria. His involvement in politics in support of the revolution did not last for long. Having gained insight into the aims and ways of 'Hayaat Al-Tahreer' -run in Alexandria by Nasser's brother El Laithy- which he disapproved of, he and his colleagues withdrew from political activities. Later, he iterated that President Nasser's policies are likely to negatively impact developments in Egypt for decades in the future.

President Nasser was a well meaning nationalist. However, his actions on the whole led to many unintended but unfortunate consequences.

He was aware of the plight of the Egyptian farmer, and was a confirmed socialist. One of his first moves was to strip the ownership of land from the largest feudal owners and to distribute the confiscated land among the farmers who toiled it. This while comprehensible, was not well planned and led to serious losses in the efficiency of producing crops, and thus to negative impacts on Egypt's economy.

Another act led to much graver consequences. In his move to consolidate his power, he appointed members of the military to control nearly all facets of development in the country. Most ministers of government and the heads of governmental institutions were military officers. Major private enterprises were nationalized and their CEOs were replaced with military officers. Alas, the military were often ineffective in managing fields outside of their military expertise.

A milestone development of the Nasser era relates to the construction of the Aswan High Dam. President Nasser viewed the implementation of the project as a national priority. The Nile River is prone to annual cycles of flooding and relative water scarcity, as well as the recurring episodes of Biblical renown relating to water abundance and droughts that last for years on end; all depending on the amount of rain that falls at the Nile's sources upstream to the South. The dam was conceived to create a lake reservoir that would allow regulating the flow of water both annually and long term, and to generate electricity as well.

However, the project was criticized by many Egyptian engineers. Prominent among them was Dr. Abdel Aziz Ahmed, a cousin of my father. He was the Chairman of the Hydro Electric Commission of Egypt at the time, and a senior member of both the Institution of Electrical Engineers and the Institution of Civil Engineers in London. He pointed out that several serious negative environmental consequences would ensue from building the dam. He also indicated that the benefits sought could be achieved by other less expensive and less environmentally damaging means. President Nasser did not heed the advice of the experts. I was aware of these developments in my boyhood. My father made a point of taking me with him on many occasions to formal and informal meetings where the issues were debated. The debate over the advantages and disadvantages of the Aswan High Dam still lingers today.

President Nasser, bent on implementing his dream for Egypt sought financing from Western Powers. John Foster Dulles, US Foreign Secretary at the time, first promised to assist, then later reneged on his promise. Under pressure particularly from the USA, the World Bank withdrew its offer to finance the construction of the High Dam. This drove Nasser to seek financing from the Soviet Union who indulged him. These developments ushered an era of Egyptian cooperation with the USSR, and a rift with Western Powers; a landmark development that impacted conditions in Egypt as well as the Middle East region at large.

President Nasser also tended to be confrontational in conducting foreign policy. In response to the withdrawal of the World Bank offer to finance the Aswan High Dam, he nationalized the Suez Canal in 1956; an act that provided an excuse for military action by the UK, France, and Israel.

I was about to graduate from college at the time and volunteered with the rest of my class to join the National Guard to fend off the attackers; my father did not approve! It took the government sometime to provide us with uniforms and rifles, and some rudimentary training. Then we were moved to one university building for use as a barrack. What sticks in my mind is that one afternoon we learned that the British dropped leaflets indicating that they intended to bomb that particular building. Discussing this rumor with our 'superiors', we were told that we are strictly prohibited from leaving the building. Perhaps we were being used as human shields; if so, the ploy worked since the building was not bombed. At any rate this episode lasted only for a few weeks after which we were disbanded, when President Eisenhower interfered to stop the attack on Egypt. However, some of my close school class mates were killed in the invasion; notably, a navy officer on an Egyptian torpedo boat that was sunk in the Mediterranean, and a dear friend whose mother was English, who volunteered to serve and was killed in the Suez Canal area.

Israel's joining the UK and France in the invasion of the Suez Canal area in 1956 to punish President Nasser for nationalizing the strategic waterway, and to squash the potential rise of Egypt as a regional power, had important ramifications. Nasser mounted a campaign against the local Jewish community, and the Egyptian people's consideration of 'the Jewish people' as an 'enemy' amplified. This led to further polarization of Moslems and Jews. Many Jewish families left the country, while some with deep roots elected to stay.

I graduated with distinction as an architect from the University of Alexandria in 1957; I was 21years old. This entitled me to apply for a scholarship to do graduate work. Following in my father's footsteps I was appointed lecturer and later received the scholarship to pursue graduate studies at Harvard. The scholarship was subsequently changed to my father's alma mater, the FIT, Zurich. I left for Zurich in January, 1959.

In spite of prevailing negative developments, my life in Alexandria was rewarding and pleasurable. I recall that I was reluctant to leave Egypt. It took some persuasion form my father and my professors to convince me to accept the scholarship in Switzerland.

I returned to Egypt in April 1959 for one month to be married, and traveled back to Zurich with my wife. Two years later in

January, 1961 I was qualified by the FIT to prepare a doctoral thesis. My wife and I returned to Egypt with our son for a vacation that was supposed not to exceed tow moths. President Nasser was in power, and we noticed a marked deterioration in many aspects of life. However, I stayed in Egypt for three months which I thoroughly enjoyed.

My wife remained in Egypt with our son to pursue her university degree which was interrupted by our marriage and departure to Switzerland. After obtaining her degree in English Literature, she had a horrific time dealing with Egyptian authorities to allow her to rejoin me in Switzerland; a sign of the restrictions on travel that were getting worse with time.

In the nineteen sixties as conditions continued to deteriorate in Egypt, my father together with many prominent colleagues from the University of Alexandria went to Libya during King Idris Al-Senussi's reign to establish a college of engineering in Tripoli; I visited the family there for a week in 1965. My father lived in Tripoli for a number of years, returned to teach in Egypt, and then later went to Syria to teach at the University of Aleppo, and then back to teach in Egypt until he passed away in 1972. During the latter years of his life, Egypt had evolved into a police state. My father was outspoken in his criticism of the regime. However, he was so popular that the authorities did not dare to harm him. At any rate, he advised me not to return to Egypt. I thought if my father with his deep roots and distinguished stature and career in Egypt elected to leave the country on several occasions, how could I hope for a meaningful future in Egypt?

Over the years, President Nasser indulged in rhetorical statements antagonizing the USA and Israel, which he was not in a position to back up with meaningful action. This again provided an excuse for Israel to attack Egypt in a 'preemptive strike' in June, 1967, which lasted for six days and resulted in the loss of substantial Arab territories to Israel. The lost lands included the Sinai

Peninsula, the Golan Heights, the West Bank, East Jerusalem, and the Gaza Strip; lands that the Arabs tried to regain since then. These territories were lost in a jiffy as a result of Israel's aggression which took advantage of President Nasser's rhetoric and to the ineptness of certain Egyptian military generals at the time.

This most regrettable development is referred to in the Arab world as "al naxah", i.e. the setback. And what a setback! The chief of the Egyptian military Marshal Abdel Hakim Aamer committed suicide within a few weeks; by some accounts he was 'suicided'. President Nasser himself died heartbroken a few years thereafter.

President Nasser also had geopolitical aspirations. For example, he sent Egyptian troops to Yemen in a costly but failed military campaign in an attempt to influence internal political affairs there. He was also abusively critical of some Arab leaders in ways that compromised Egypt's relations with neighboring countries including Syria and Saudi Arabia.

I do not wish to leave the reader with a negative impression of President Nasser's contributions. On the positive side he was instrumental in liberating the oppressed Egyptian farmer, and in ending the British occupation of Egypt. Also, he was acutely aware of the machinations of imperial capitalism and collaborated with Presidents Nehru of India and Tito of Yugoslavia in forming the Non-aligned Nations Movement that tried to counter the influence of Western Powers. What I wish to confirm though is that major mistakes were made in the pursuit of revolutionary goals which led to grave setbacks in developments both in Egypt and other Arab countries. Israel and Western Powers were definitely culprit in bringing about these negative developments. On the whole though, my father's concerns over Egypt's future after the 1952 revolution were justified.

Israel's action in the six day war confirmed it as a real enemy of the Egyptian people. This event had the gravest consequences in aggravating the polarization of Moslems and Jews, and to the mushrooming of radical Islamism in Egypt, and beyond.

The humiliation that all Egyptians felt after the 1967 six day war with Israel sealed my decision not to return to Egypt. I decided to immigrate to Canada. I arrived in Toronto in November, 1967. My wife and two children born in Zurich joined me there a few months later. In addition to the harsh winter weather in Canada, economic conditions at the time were not favorable to new immigrants. We immigrated to the USA in August 1970. These personal decisions can be readily related to the changing conditions in Egypt.

Before we immigrated to the USA, I took a trip with my family to find a job in the US. We stopped in Boston, New York City, and New Jersey where I had close friends. Two firms, both owned by Jewish architects, one in New York City and one in New Jersey offered me a job. I accepted the offer in NJ and worked with the firm for a year. After working on short assignments with a couple of other NJ firms, I worked with a Jewish architect for three and half years -the longest period that I have ever 'worked for others'- before getting my architectural license in NJ and starting my own practice. Later on, I was offered a partnership to practice with two firms both owned by Jewish colleagues.

When we moved to the US we rented a house in Watchung, NJ. We bought the house next door after one year. In Watchung, I met a Jewish neighbor, the late Dr. Bernie Struhl who became my friend, dentist, and tennis partner. Bernie and I won the local tennis doubles tournament! Many of those I played tennis with in the US over the years were Jewish. Most of the medical doctors I see on a regular basis are Jewish.

The above facts illustrate my attitude towards Jewish people in general, and the attitudes of the Jewish people whom I had occasion to interact with in my life. The facts reflect mutual respect based on personal appreciation and professional merit. I make a point of mentioning these facts in order to avert recrimination by some who might be tempted to dub me as 'anti-Semitic'. Please save your breath and mine: I am not.

After President Nasser's death, Anwar Sadat -a close confidant of Nasser- became President in October 1970. He remained in power until he was assassinated in October 1981.

President Sadat, a more pragmatic statesman compared with President Nasser who tended to be more idealistic, was able to wage a successful attack on Israel's fortifications in the occupied Sinai along the Eastern edge of the Suez Canal on the 6th of October, 1973. He demonstrated that Egypt was not to be regarded as a pushover insignificant country. Working with President Jimmy Carter later on, they forged a peace agreement between Egypt and Israel that returned Egypt's sovereignty over the Sinai. By his astute action to regain the Sinai, he restored pride and dignity to the Egyptian people.

In parallel with the above developments between Egypt and Israel, the Israeli occupation of Palestinian lands acquired in the six day war, and Israel's harsh treatment of the Palestinian people in general attracted international attention and condemnation of Israel. The resolution of the Palestinian issue was internationally recognized as cardinal to attaining regional peace. President Sadat, being fully aware of these circumstances, and being sympathetic with the Palestinian cause, made sure that the resolution of the Palestinian issue was covered as a key component of the provisions of the peace agreement between Egypt and Israel.

Alas, Prime Minister Menachem Begin, the Israeli signatory to the agreement, reneged on the implementation of the peace agreement's provisions regarding the Palestinian issue. This understandably added more fuel to the rift between Israel, and Egypt and Arabs and Moslems in general, and to buttressing radical religious movements that warned about dealing with Israel through negotiation, and advocated instead an armed struggle against Israel.

In my view, President Sadat was a great statesman who set forth to rectify many of the negative consequences of Nasserism. He reinstituted a multi-party system, and launched "Al Infitah" referred to as the "Open Door" economic policy to encourage foreign investment in Egypt.

After visiting Egypt in 1961, I did not set foot there again until 1976, well after President Sadat assumed power. My father had passed away. I learned about his death several weeks after the fact. My family did not inform me immediately for fear that had I returned to attend my father's funeral I might have been prevented from leaving the country. Over the 15 years of my absence, the country had physically deteriorated almost beyond recognition.

When it was pointed out to President Nasser that his policies are leading to an exodus of intellectuals and a brain drain out of Egypt to other countries, his response was: we do not need these people, let them go. President Sadat on the other hand invited Egyptian expatriates to return and participate in rebuilding the country. Many took up his invitation.

Between 1976 and late 1979 I used to travel on professional business between the USA and Egypt on a regular basis. I was elated by the prospect of getting involved and assisting in Egypt's recovery. My brothers and I operating out of the US were involved in a privately funded project to prepare a master plan for a new town for a 100,000 population. We also joint ventured with other US firms to pursue two major US AID sponsored projects. The first was to define the national urban policy for the whole of Egypt, and the second to study the development of the Sinai Peninsula. Based on technical evaluation of our proposals to provide the required professional services, we tied for second place on the first project, and tied for first place on the second. Unfortunately for us, other competing US firms were awarded the contracts for these significant projects.

The loss of the AID projects led me to seek other professional assignments. These took me to Kuwait from 1980 to 1986 where I was involved in several major architectural projects. I returned to practice in the US and stayed here until 1991.

During my stay in the US I served on a short UN assignment to Libya during President Gaddafi's presidency. Soon thereafter I got another UN assignment for one year to Qatar at the time the country was preparing for the exploitation of its enormous gas resources. The UN assignment in Qatar led to other private professional engagements in Dubai, and Saudi Arabia, after which I returned to Qatar as an in house advisor to the Planning Department there. I returned to practice in the US in 2006. From 1980 to date I returned to Egypt occasionally only for personal business or as a tourist.

In 1975, President Sadat appointed Air Force General Hosni Mubarak as his Vice President. Mubarak took over as President after Sadat's assassination in 1981. Egypt's economy tended to improve during his close to thirty year presidency, especially through the development of Egypt's touristic resources. However, he was accused of running the country as a private business, and reserving business opportunities to his immediate family and clan; the gap between rich and poor was growing.

On December18, 2010 demonstrations erupted in Tunisia. They were sparked by an incident the previous day in which a twenty- six-year -old man, Mohamed Bouazizi set himself on fire in protest against his ruthless and undignified treatment by local authorities. The incident led to a campaign of civil resistance in the face of intolerable conditions of poverty, unemployment, lack of civil liberties, and corruption in Tunisia, and led to the ouster of then President Bin Ali.

Events in Tunisia inspired the Egyptian people to revolt against the rule of President Hosni Mubarak. Poverty and unemployment were among the main factors that led to a popular revolution on January 25, 2011, and ultimately to President Mubarak's ouster on February 11. President Mubarak's VP Omar Suleiman announced Mubarak's resignation and the transfer of power to the Armed Forces Supreme Council headed by Marshal Tantawi. This seemed to be a preliminary step towards a potential 'change of the guard'.

The revolts in Tunisia and Egypt were followed by similar revolts in Libya and other countries in the region which are now dubbed "the Arab spring".

The Egyptian people whose uprising forced President Mubarak to resign continued their pressure on the government through public demonstrations to hold national elections. The government conceded to hold a referendum that took place on March 19, 2011. Parliamentary elections followed and Islamist groups won a majority of seats in the parliament. However, the High Constitutional Court declared the elections unconstitutional, and dissolved the Parliament. Later on, early in 2013 national presidential elections effectively brought an old often persecuted Egyptian institution, the Moslem Brotherhood (MB) to assume the reins of power in the country.

No account of contemporary Egypt is complete without covering the history of the MB. The group was founded in 1928 by Hassan Al-Banna, a Moslem scholar and schoolteacher. The group's stated goal is to establish the Quran -Islam's equivalent of the Torah and the Bible- and the Sunnah -a set of rules derived from Prophet Mohammed's statements and teachings- as the basis for individual, social, and state conduct. The movement which gained acceptance and followers over the years in many Arab and Moslem countries functioned often as a sort of an NGO providing sundry social services to the needy. However, from its inception, the group expressed and demonstrated its willingness and intent to use lethal force whenever necessary to attain its goals.

A series of assassinations and attempts of assassination of prominent Egyptian leaders have been attributed to the MB: notably the assassination of prominent political leaders in the forties, including Prime Minister Mahmoud Al-Nukrashi in Cairo in 1948, the attempted assassination of President Nasser in Alexandria in 1954, and the actual assassination of President Sadat in Cairo in 1981. It is noteworthy that the founder of the MB Hassan Al-Banna, was himself assassinated a few weeks after the assassination of Prime Minister Nukrashi.

The MB has been reviled and feared by the rulers of Egypt starting with administrations under King Farouk, and throughout those under Presidents Nasser, Sadat, and Mubarak; with brief reprieves during the Sadat and Mubarak presidencies. This resulted in occasional banning of the organization's activities, and the arrest and imprisonment of many MB members and leaders over the past decades. In spite of oppression, the MB succeeded in maintaining its organization and continued to pursue its ends.

It is to be noted that the growth of the MB's popularity in Egypt and elsewhere in the ME could be in part related to Israel's actions. Al Qaeda's expressed views regarding Israel, and the fact that Anwar Al Zawaheri, Bin Laden's first lieutenant is an MB leader attest to that.

The MB came to power after two rounds of presidential elections that were held after the ouster of President Mubarak: the first in May 2012 among five major candidates, and the second in June among the two leading candidates of the first round, namely, General Ahmed Shafik a former Prime Minister, and Mohammed Morsi affiliated with the MB. Mohammed Morsi won in the second round.

Although the Egyptian Constitution since the early days of President Sadat allowed for a multi party system, in practice, the National Democratic Party (NDP) loyal to the military continued for decades to be the sole effective political party in the country. Thus, when the presidential elections of 2012 took place, there were only two organized entities in the country in a position to compete effectively, the NDP which the people perceived as representing the old regime they were trying to get rid of, and the MB which never had any experience in running the country.

Many who wanted mainly to get rid of the remnants of the old regime, perhaps reluctantly, voted for Mr. Morsi. He won with 51.7% of the vote. I am convinced that his success related more to the fact that the MB were relatively better organized compared with other nascent political entities, and to the votes of those who mainly wanted to avoid the return of the old military regime. Thus, although the MB has a large constituency, Mr. Morsi's election as President did not necessarily mean that a majority of the Egyptian people are fully sympathetic with the MB.

Shortly after his election, it became clear that President Morsi was receiving instructions on a regular almost daily basis from the 'Morshed' -i.e. religious leader- of the MB Mr. Badie, who seemed to be actually running the country Iranian style! The intent of the new regime was confirmed by President Morsi's rush to institute a new Constitution that prescribed that the laws of the land are to be inspired by Islamic Sharia Law. Running the country in the absence of an elected parliament, President Morsi moved forcefully to consolidate the MB's grip on power and to institutionalize the MB's Islamist views. Particularly noteworthy, he issued a Decree immunizing his decisions from future judicial challenge.

This act among others, led to massive protests in December 2012 which involved widespread clashes between his supporters and opponents. President Morsi resisted all efforts of rapprochement by his opponents. His liberal opponents having had enough of the MB's ways, and fearing that the MB's agenda will be impossible to reverse if the MB were allowed to remain in power for the remaining three years of President Morsi's tenure, planned, organized and pre-announced a popular uprising on June 30, 2013 asking President Morsi to step down. By some accounts 30 million opponents of Morsi showed up. President Morsi's response to this event was defiant. The army saw an opportunity to ally itself with the liberal secularists, and deposed President Morsi three days later on July 3 in what some insist to call a coup d'état, while others call a democratic revolt; or the people's second revolution. Note that the Egyptian Constitution had no provisions for impeaching President Morsi.

The MB's response was both frantic and violent. They organized protracted counter demonstrations, incited violence against Egyptian Copts and Shia Moslems, and attacked police and security forces; tens of Coptic churches were burned and looted. The police with the army's support responded forcefully. The toll that ensued amounted to a thousand Egyptians killed and several thousand injured.

The Chairman of the High Constitutional Court was installed as an interim President, and a government was put in place by the military after the ouster of President Morsi. The appointed government was entrusted with the task of conceiving a road map for future action. The interim government formed two committees of political figures, and legal experts to write a new Constitution. The new Constitution was adopted by national referendum in January 2014.

MB sabotaging activities continued especially in the Sinai. The assassination of the Minister of Interior was attempted but failed. The interim government in its efforts to restore security and stability in the country felt compelled to outlaw the MB organization.

Later on presidential elections were held, and General Abdel Fattah El Sisi -former head of military intelligence- was elected President in June 2014 with an overwhelming majority over one other candidate who ran against him. Shortly before the presidential elections, the interim government resigned and was replaced by another. Upon his election President El Sisi formed a new government retaining the former Prime Minister and a few key ministers. Parliamentary elections were scheduled to be held in December 2014. However, elections were postponed to March 2015, and then postponed again for judicial reasons. They are now scheduled to be held perhaps in June 2015.

As feared, the new government clamped down on most forms of opposition. This seems to have helped in curtailing the MB's sabotaging activities. Although scattered terrorist incidents still occur, security and stability may be slowly returning to the country.

The country's economic conditions remain to be dire in spite of the infusion of 12 billion dollars by Saudi Arabia, the United Arab Emirates (UAE), Kuwait, and Bahrain. The new government though has embarked on an ambitious program of economic development; including a major project to increase the capacity of the Suez Canal, as well as numerous substantial housing projects. In mid March 2015 the government organized an economic conference to attract international investors to Egypt. The conference was well attended and succeeded in soliciting pledges for investment totaling over 100 billion Dollars over the next five to ten years.

When I visited Egypt recently in early 2013, I observed the contrast between pockets of upscale projects scattered within a sea of shanty like development. This reminded me of one of the hottest issues that were debated while I lived in Egypt.

The population of Egypt before I left in 1959 was less than 30 million but growing rapidly. Many warned that rapid population growth will have ominous consequences, since more people will have to share the countries' relatively limited resources. Therefore, population growth has to be contained. This warning was not heeded. The population now is around 90 million.

Consecutive Egyptian administrations under King Farouk, and Presidents Nasser, Sadat, and Mubarak sometimes attempted, but ultimately failed to implement effective measures to slow down population growth, or otherwise, develop the countries resources to accommodate the needs of the millions of the growing population beyond mere survival levels. The accumulated results of failure in this respect are becoming progressively more evident, and constitute a major factor that contributed to the emergence of recent upheavals in Egypt.

Conclusion

The event that had the most ominous and far reaching impact on developments in Egypt was the creation of the State of Israel. Four wars ensued from this event, in 1948, 1956, 1967, and 1973. In addition to human losses, these wars directed substantial resources towards military spending instead of badly needed internal economic development. Israel's emergence also profoundly impacted political developments in Egypt by initiating events that triggered the 1952 revolution as recounted above.

Furthermore, and perhaps most importantly, the creation and subsequent action of the State of Israel led to the polarization of Jews and Moslems in Egypt, and contributed to the spread of Islamist sentiments both in Egypt and the Middle East.

When I lived in Egypt, very few women wore the 'hejab'; the traditional Moslem head cover. Now a majority of women, and girls, do. This is but one example reflecting the growth of the constituency of the Moslem Brotherhood and religious Islamist sentiments in general which resulted, at least partially, from the creation and action of the State of Israel. This issue will be further discussed in the following chapter.

Perhaps one benefit to the Egyptian people that might be ascribed to the creation of the State of Israel is the US's financial aid to Egypt which started in 1973 after signing the Peace Accords with Israel, to encourage Egypt to maintain its peace with Israel! Please note in this context that the US for decades, has been providing Israel with military gear to the tune of several billion Dollars a year free of charge, thus establishing Israel as the preeminent military power in the Middle East.

Imperial Powers must share responsibility in the creation of negative conditions in Egypt. The British invaded and occupied the country, and attacked the Suez Canal jointly with the French and Israelis. Furthermore, Western Powers including the USA aided and abetted in the creation and sustenance of the State of Israel leading to the detrimental consequences discussed above.

Action by the Egyptian People and their Leaders also contributed to the evolution of negative conditions. Dire economic conditions reflected in high percentages of poverty and unemployment, and human rights abuses in recent decades have certainly contributed to the emergence of discontent and strife in Egypt.

The political leaders of the country bear responsibility for this. It seems to me that leaders such as Mohammed Ali and Sadat brought about predominantly positive conditions. Other political leaders are responsible in various degrees for a mixed bag of both positive and negative developments.

Religious leaders also influenced developments. Al Azhar, Egypt's renowned Islamic Institution maintained a centric position which tended to promote stability in the country. On the other hand, the leaders of the Moslem Brotherhood while contributing positively in certain ways can be blamed for frequently inciting violence. This is evidenced in the MB's involvement for decades in the assassination of political leaders, and more recently in acts of violence against Copts and Shia Moslems, and continuing terrorist acts in response to deposing former President Morsi.

The Egyptian people themselves share responsibility for their predicament. The most glaring example of negative action is the assassination by Moslem fanatics of President Sadat, the man who restored Egypt's valor, especially, when compared with the popular uproar urging President Nasser not to resign after the 'Naxah'. The people affected developments by their action and by their choice of leaders whenever possible, and by the extent of support or rejection of those in power. Having been mostly ruled by authoritarian regimes their input was relatively limited. However, since the Arab Spring the Egyptian people have demonstrated exemplary courage and resolve in a series of attempts to define their destiny.

I was in Cairo in January 2015 for a short visit. Apart from staunch MB supporters, the prevailing mood among many seems to reflect reserved acceptance of current political conditions, combined with an attitude of 'wait and see'. Some advice!

Egyptians like other peoples in the world, seek freedom, dignity, and social justice. Also, a large majority aspire to improve their financial lot. Attaining these goals requires vigorous economic development and predicates the prevalence of security and stability in the country.

The leaders of the Egyptian revolution conceived a road map for progress. It is being implemented in a seemingly judicious and timely fashion. A new Constitution promoting secularity and respect of human rights was crafted according to schedule, and presidential elections took place in 2014.

The new government in parallel, and in spite of the difficult conditions perpetrated by MB radical entities, is rigorously addressing the economic woes of the country through concerted development programs. Thankfully, Saudi Arabia, the United Arab Emirates, Kuwait, and Bahrain have generously contributed in this effort. This is evidence of their sympathy with Egypt's stance vis-à-vis radical Islamism. The road ahead however is flowed with obstacles.

The MB no doubt has a large constituency of sympathizers. Furthermore, some of the MB's leaders and followers are radical fanatics who are indoctrinated to use lethal violence to attain whatever goals they deem appropriate from their egocentric perspective. They resisted all attempts for reconciliation and reverted instead to violently assail their opponents. They burned churches, attempted to assassinate the Minister of Interior, and created havoc in the Sinai and many other areas of the country. The continuing violent reaction to losing power reveals the MB's true mettle, and the resulting instability is negatively impacting tourism and economic development in general. This is forcing the new government to adopt counter measures to contain the MB's aggression. Sorting out the issues relating to the MB will continue to constitute a major obstacle in the way of progress. Therefore, the first piece of advice that I will offer is concerned with addressing this issue.

The new government in its efforts to restore security and stability in the country was recently compelled to disband the MB organization. At this stage one can hardly expect that Mr. Morsi could be possibly reinstated as President, or that the MB with its former leadership could reassume power. Developments have already progressed far beyond such potentialities. The MB had a chance to run the affairs of Egypt. The approach they adopted turned a large majority of Egyptians against them. Continuing their relentless assault on their perceived opponents, in addition to hurting the country as a whole, is certainly leading ever more people to disapprove of their methods. This will compromise any chances they might have had to participate in future political developments.

Therefore, the MB's rank and file are well advised to reconsider their position in light of reality, rather than continue to pursue unrealistic goals and objectives. Above all, they are advised to control the radicals amongst them, and cease and desist from mounting further terrorist acts. Doing so is in their best long term interest and the interest of the whole country as well.

Former members of the MB could reorganize by choosing new leaders and formulating a new moderate secularist agenda that recognizes and avoids the pitfalls learned from past experience. This would pave the way for their participation in future political developments. The new government initially endorsed this proposition, and is advised to continue to encourage those who would oblige in true democratic spirit. Recent developments however, caused by the MB's intransigence, seem to preclude the realization of such hopes in the near future.

Since the incarceration of former MB members and leaders will remain to be a sticky issue for some time, the government is advised to avoid handling matters with an attitude of revenge, but rather in a restrained and humane manner. We need though to put ourselves in President El Sisi's shoes.

When Mr. Obama became president over six years ago, he seemed to have an admirable agenda which he proceeded to implement. His achievements fall short of the expectations of many of his supporters; the midterm elections of November 4, 2014 reflect general dissatisfaction with the Democratic Party. Perhaps he had to contend with grave issues inherited from the preceding administration which influenced and curtailed his efforts.

Likewise, from day one, President El Sisi has been facing existential issues threatening the Egyptian national identity. His main challenge is to establish security and stability as necessary to be in a position to pursue rigorous economic development. Malicious entities are constantly challenging his efforts. For example, in late October 2014 an unidentified group of militias mounted an orchestrated attack on a road check point near Rafah in the Sinai that killed and injured 60 Egyptian soldiers. Similar terrorist acts are being committed as I prepare to go to print in mid April 2015. Such incidents are forcing, and will continue to force the government to take harsh and sometimes unpopular measures to contain and apprehend the perpetrators.

Another potentially negative issue relates to the military's attitudes in the way of consolidating power, and to their true intentions not to return to pre-revolution conditions. The manner of deposing former President Morsi sent the wrong message to some Egyptians who abhor the prospect of returning to military rule, and provided an opportunity to others who were waiting for an excuse to criticize the Egyptian revolution. Also, the incarceration of news media reporters, and the passing of whole sale death sentences on MB members, cannot be condoned. Some measures relating to the freedom of expression and civil rights might be tolerated in light of the internal and external adversarial activities that aim to hamper progress. However, the government will hopefully gradually ease up restrictions and lead the country to an exemplary form of secular democracy. President El Sisi is urged to do what he can under the present circumstances to ease people's minds in these respects.

The Egyptian experience generally echoes the main issues that prevailed in the ME region in recent decades. They relate to the creation and subsequent action of the State of Israel, to incursions by Western Powers, and to the action of local Arab populations and their leaders. The following three chapters are concerned with confirming this proposition and addressing the roots of issues.

Chapter 2

ISRAEL'S CULPABILITY AND POTENTIAL ACTION

Looking at the map of the ME, it is not difficult to conceive that the forced injection of Zionist immigrants from Europe, Russia, and other parts of the world in the center of the predominantly Moslem region must have influenced developments in profound ways.

I cited the lethal conflicts between Egypt and Israel and their consequences. Likewise, similar conditions evolved in parallel affecting other ME countries and peoples. First and foremost among them are the Palestinian people who have experienced enduring devastating conditions for over six decades that still prevail at present.

By their own admission, Zionist leaders intended to 'colonize' Palestine. Their quest led to decades of turmoil in Palestine in the early 19 hundreds, followed by a war in 1948 that neighboring Arab countries waged in an effort to help the Palestinians. Egyptian, Jordanian, Lebanese, Syrian, and other Arab forces were involved in the war; I mentioned my father's initial attitude to cooperate with Jewish immigrants, and how he later changed his position.

The war of 1948 is referred to as "The War of Independence" by the Israelis, and "Al Nakbah" or "The Catastrophe" by the Arabs. The war ended with the signing of Armistice Agreements which gave Israel more land than had been foreseen by the international community, and to the declaration of the State of Israel. It also resulted in giving Egypt control over the Gaza Strip, and allowing Jordan to control of the West Bank; I also mentioned how this debacle triggered the events that eventually led to the military revolution of 1952 in Egypt.

Although many Jewish settlers were killed in their effort to establish a Jewish State, many more Palestinians were slaughtered during the initial phases of the creation of the State of Israel. Ultimately 85% of Arab Palestinians were either driven out of their homes or otherwise left the country in fear for their lives. Many fled to neighboring Arab countries, some of whom have been living in refugee camps since then in Jordan, Lebanon, and Syria. Those who managed to stay in their home land lived in East Jerusalem, the West Bank, and the Gaza Strip which were separated by the newly created State of Israel.

In 1967 Israel waged its 'preemptive' war against Egypt, Jordan, and Syria which lasted for six days. The war resulted in Israel's occupation of the Sinai, the Golan Heights, East Jerusalem, and the West Bank. Thus, the Palestinians who lived in East Jerusalem and the West Bank came under Israeli occupation.

Gaza remained as the only area where Palestinians were not living under Israeli occupation. However, in 2008 Israel occupied Gaza for about a year before withdrawing after destroying Palestinian homes and major components of the infrastructure. Israel mounted a series of assaults on the Gaza strip over the years, the last of which in July/August 2014, in each round killing and injuring thousands of Palestinians, and destroying property and infrastructure. Israel also imposes a permanent siege on Gaza, effectively incarcerating its residents.

East Jerusalem and the West Bank are recognized internationally as occupied Palestinian lands. Israel exercises the power of an occupier over all sorts of developments in these territories. Furthermore, it continues to confiscate Palestinian lands to build new Jewish settlements in defiance of international law. It is building a wall separating the lands it carves out from the rest of the occupied territories, and is claiming water resources leaving the Palestinians in critical water-poverty conditions.

Israel invaded Lebanon in 1982, and attacked Syria during that invasion. One of its main objectives was to oust the Palestinians out of Lebanon. Israeli forces formed a siege around the Capital Beirut to force the refugees out of the city. A multinational force of American, French, and Italian troops joined later by British troops, were called in to supervise the evacuation of the Palestinians. A series of violent incidents involving all parties, instead of driving the Palestinians out of Beirut, led to mass killing of Palestinians inside their Sabra and Shatila refugee camp. Israel continued to occupy large areas of southern Lebanon until the year 2000.

In their efforts to organize themselves politically the Palestinians formed the Palestine Liberation Organization (PLO) in 1964. Initially, the PLO's goal was to liberate Palestine from Israeli occupation through armed struggle. Over many years of transformation the PLO created the political party Fatah which recognizes Israel's right to existence.

Fatah has limited authority in the West Bank. They have attempted to make peace with Israel over the past decades to no avail; in my view due to Israel's intransigence. This led to the emergence of the radical Islamist group Hamas which is affiliated with the MB to assume control of the government in Gaza. They came to power through open democratic elections; in a way similar to the rise of the MB in Egypt. Hamas promoted armed struggle in view of the failure of Fatah's negotiating efforts with Israel; this incurred Israel's wrath on Gaza.

More recently however, in an effort to join Fatah in reviving the stalled peace negotiations with Israel, Hamas indicated its willingness to reconsider its expressed belligerent position towards Israel. Alas, Israel did not respond favorably to Fatah and Hamas's bid to resume peace negotiations. This led to the lethal conflict between Israel and Hamas in Gaza in July/August, 2014 which claimed the lives of 2,000 Palestinians, and over 70 Israelis.

The incidents cited above exemplify the turmoil that ensued from the creation of the State of Israel in the midst of the Middle East. Several other incidents of lethal conflicts and wars exerted a heavy toll on Israel's neighbors, and influenced political developments in the region. In addition, Israel's creation also had serious ideological ramifications.

While some incidents of the conflicts between Israel and its neighbors were instigated by the Arabs, as for example numerous skirmishes initiated by the Palestinians, and the 1973 war initiated by Egypt, others were instigated by Israel, most notably the 1967 'preemptive' war against Egypt, Jordan, and Syria.

Irrespective however, past engagements reflect a glaring asymmetry, with Israel holding a progressively overwhelming balance of power over its adversaries and thus, inflicting considerably more damage on its foes than what it incurs from their action. Thus, as Israel engaged in lethal conflicts with its neighbors, and as it continued its harsh treatment of the Palestinians, other Arab and Moslem peoples observed developments with trepidation. Each incident of Israeli humiliation of Arabs, who are predominantly Moslem, sent shock waves that propagated outward in all directions to reach the farthest removed of Moslem peoples and countries.

Over more than six decades these waves progressively led to ever more radicalization of Moslem populations around the globe; the emergence of Al Qaeda and its action on 9/11 is but one example that demonstrates this proposition. Thus, in addition to loss of life, sapping economic resources, and negatively impacting internal political developments in neighboring countries, the creation of the Nation State of Israel on religious grounds released the genie of religious radicalism in the ME and around the world. Israel's subsequent action contributed to the widespread of radical Islamism and its consequences which are manifested the crisis that we are witnessing today.

On October 5, 2014 Fareed Zachariah interviewed Israel's Prime Minister Benjamin Netanyahu on CNN's program GPS. Netanyahu described the current problems with radical Islamist groups, and pointed out that his government cannot deal with such entities. This is reminiscent of the case of a bully who keeps repeatedly abusing his victim and inciting the victim to stand up and fight. If the victim reacts to being abused, he is blamed for being an aggressive nasty guy. If the victim pleads for reconciliation, his pleas are dismissed as not deserving of recognition! Thus, a fundamental question was not raised in the interview of Prime Minister Netanyahu, namely: how did conditions evolve in the Middle East to get us to where we are today? I hope that my discourse will help in answering this question.

No doubt, Western Imperial Powers played a critical role in the evolution of the above negative conditions. They are culprit in their initiation and materialization as will be explained in the following chapter.

While sympathetic with the Jewish People and understanding of the many atrocious circumstances they endured over the centuries that led to their desire to have a country of their own, I have a basic concern regarding the notion of creating a 'Jewish Nation State' in the modern world, let alone in the midst of the ME region. I harbor the same concerns over the creation of a 'Christian State' or an 'Islamic State'.

The term "Jewish State" literally reflects departure from the concept of 'the separation of church and state' which was conceived by the French, and introduced by Thomas Jefferson in the First Amendment to the Constitution of the United States; he referred to it as the "absolute wall of separation between church and state". The extent of separation, and the merits and demerits of the concept have been debated over the decades. My position in this respect relates to my understanding of monotheist religions, and to the attitudes of some of the radical pious. It is fully expressed in chapter 5.

That religious people may elect to pray once a week or five times a day is their privilege. If they elect to conduct their respective weekly prayers in a synagogue on the Sabbath, in a church on Sunday or in a Mosque on Friday is also their privilege. However, while respectful of the rights of all to worship according to their beliefs, I certainly do not condone any move by religious groups to impose their often contradictory preferences regarding individual and social behavior on others; especially fundamental groups that espouse literal or biased interpretations of their respective scriptures, which usually entail detrimental consequences. In my view, any group of people whether Jewish, Christian, or Moslem that attempts to do that cannot be entrusted with the conduct of state affairs.

Now, Zionism is predicated on the presumption that all lands between the Euphrates and the Nile belong to the Israelites. Thus, some Israelis believe that they have a divine right to acquire ever more Palestinian lands, and perhaps continue their quest until they reach the Euphrates and the Nile. As mentioned earlier tough, many Jewish scholars consider this attitude to have resulted from a biased interpretation of the Torah. The Zionist attitude also reflects disregard of the fact that other peoples happen to be living on these lands at present. Israel's wars and land acquisitions did indeed entail detrimental consequences on others. This is evidence of how biased religious beliefs often instigate trouble, and demonstrates the need to generally avoid the involvement of religious zealots in the affairs of state.

These considerations constitute my objection, by principle, to the creation of a 'Jewish Nation State' in the modern world. It is to be noted in this context that some Evangelicals in the USA adopt biased interpretations of the Bible, and have been staunch supporters of a Greater Israel. They are referred to as 'Christian Zionists', and their attitude reflects the essence of my objection.

Obviously, the concept of the separation of religion and state is not applicable only in the case of Israel. It is equally applicable to Islamist States such as Iran, Pakistan, and Saudi Arabia who adhere to different versions of Sharia law, and generally to all contemporary Islamist movements in the ME as well. This issue will be discussed further in chapter 5.

Conclusion

Some may condone or even be pleased about the current state of affairs in the ME. Caring compassionate people do not. Many, me included, actually believe that the perpetuation of Israel's stance and strategy in the ME could prove to be detrimental to achieving its own ultimate goal of securing its future existence and prosperity in the region.

Since its inception, Israel's strategy was and continues to be to muscle its way to achieve its ulterior goals, and to change conditions on the ground to its advantage irrespective of the damaging consequences of its actions on others. To date, Israel has been on the whole quite successful in applying this strategy. However, as I have taken the effort to explain, the strategy contributed in serious ways to the evolution of the current crisis in the ME. Thus, the question arises as to what could be expected if Israel elects to continue its customary conduct?

One might hope that issues 'somehow' will sort themselves out with time to the mutual advantage of both Israel and its neighbors. This though is wishful thinking. Past experience demonstrates that Israel's strategy and action, while leading to limited net territorial gains for Israel have provoked immeasurable trouble in the region, and indignation from its neighbors who are likely to continue to find ways to get back at Israel.

The international community also seems to be recognizing that Israel's intransigence has to be addressed, and some European countries are taking steps to this end. Sweden recently officially recognized a Palestine State, and the UK and France are taking steps in this direction. Progressively over the past few years, more and more Western countries and international entities have expressed sympathy with the Palestinian cause while denouncing Israel. Also, the Palestinians have recently approached the International Criminal Court to consider the commitment of war crimes by Israel. These developments suggest that the tide of Israel's successes might be about to ebb, and that the perpetuation of its strategies could eventually backfire.

On the other hand, one could contemplate how conditions might evolve if Israel reconsiders its attitude towards its neighbors in the region. To illustrate the potential outcome of such a move I will recall a few historically significant events.

The question can be raised as to what if Prime Minister Menachem Begin did not renege on fully implementing the provisions of the Peace Accords with Egypt? What could have happened if Prime Minister Rabin was not shot by a radical right-wing Jewish assassin? What if Israel accepted the Saudi offer for peace in the region which could have paved the way for economic cooperation? More recently, Mr. Netanyahu indicated his position not to negotiate with the Palestinians as long as they remain divided into the two camps of Fatah and Hamas. When Fatah and Hamas reconciled and offered to negotiate, Mr. Netanyahu refused on account that the Palestinians have to first recognize Israel as a 'Jewish State'. From my expressed position, this brings me to square one since it reflects insistence on adhering to what I consider to be one of the roots of problems in the first place. Irrespective though, what if Mr. Netanyahu took this opportunity to start negotiating earnestly and in good faith with the Palestinians?

Obviously, it is impossible to reconstruct the past in answer to the above questions. Also, one cannot forecast the future based on the pursuit of one or the other option for subsequent action. However, one could imagine the wars, death, and destruction that could have been averted in the past, and the potential negative developments that could be possibly avoided in the future. One could also contemplate a future of peaceful coexistence and economic cooperation to the benefit of both Israel and its neighbors.

My critique of Israel is not meant to disfranchise Israel's privileges as a sovereign state. Rather, it is meant to encourage Israel to be prudent and to fundamentally reconsider and alter its political position in the ME.

Political conditions in Israel have led to a situation whereby radical religious right-wing minorities in the Knesset hold sway over critical decisions that continue to negatively impact developments in the ME. The last round of elections on March 17, 2015 confirms this proposition.

When PM Netanyahu called for the elections a few months earlier, I thought that the Israeli people could use the opportunity to contain the influence of right-wing religious minorities by electing more liberal and progressive political candidates who would be likely to alter the government's posture in prudent ways. I even felt that recent progressive movements in Tunisia and Egypt which reflect a notable move towards secularity, and the promise of economic rewards entailed in making peace with their neighbors, might encourage the Israeli electorate to change their government's attitude.

Alas, in his election campaign, Prime Minister Netanyahu averred to never allow the creation of a Palestinian state! Enough Israelis embraced his platform and granted him a fourth term in office, thus precluding any chances for reconciliation with the Palestinians for years to come.

Mr. Netanyahu did what he did in an effort to stay in power, without careful consideration of the consequences of his actions on US-Israeli relations and on the Israeli people themselves; let alone the Palestinians and other Arabs and Moslems. In my view, he elected to cling to power at any cost.

I wonder, though, how much longer Israeli right-wing politicians intend to carry on with their agenda! Perhaps they are confident that they can obliterate any and all of their potential adversaries with Israel's overwhelming nuclear power, and thus, feel that they can do what they will for as long as they wish in defiance of the world community and international law! They probably also feel that their influence over US politicians is so overwhelming, that the US will let them get away with whatever action they elect to pursue. This though raises the question: is this a sustainable strategy? And, what could one expect from the perpetuation of this strategy? The next episode of upheavals in the region could be catastrophic, and might be harmful to Israel!

One effective way to urge Israel to reconsider its posture lies in the hands of the Jewish community in the USA. The US Jewish community has been supporting Israel both financially and by applying pressure on the US government to sway its decisions to support extreme right-wing Israeli policies. If the US Jewish community is convinced that it is in Israel's best long term interest to modify its political position, the Jewish community could definitely effect developments to the benefit of Israel as well as its neighbors. Recent elections in Israel indicate that, left to its own devices, Israel may not come around to adopt the prudent strategies that many are convinced would be in its' long term benefit. This emphasizes the dire need for the Jewish community to interfere, at least, by withholding its support of extreme right-wing Israeli politicians.

Many prominent Jewish leaders and entities both in Israel and in the USA promote peace between the Israelis and the Palestinians. They have been actively trying to convince the Israelis and the US Jewish community to heed their advice for quite some time. Generally, they support a two state solution to attain peace, and recommend certain steps such as the cessation of building more unlawful Jewish settlements on Palestinian occupied territories as a crucial step in the way of reaching this goal. For their efforts, they have been referred to by some radical Zionists as "self-loathing Jews", or more civilly by others as "peaceniks". Those leaders in particular could affect developments in positive ways by continuing their constructive work.

Many Jewish leaders who promote peace, though, unfortunately from my perspective, embrace the ideology of a 'Jewish Nation State'. I doubt that meaningful change could be sought without their tacit support. Therefore, it is prudent to seek reconciliation with their sentiments.

In this vein: one could hardly ask Pakistan to renounce its status as an Islamic State, or for that matter, expect the Vatican to proclaim itself as a secular entity! Accordingly, as we continue to accept the reality of the existence of Islamist States, perhaps we need to be prepared to acknowledge a 'Jewish State'; albeit, one that would address the plight of the Palestinian people, renounce aggression, and be willing to coexist in peace with its neighbors in the region.

The prospect for the spread of secularity would still remain as the hope for the future; perhaps starting in Israel which displays higher levels of educated people and more progressive attitudes compared with other religious states in the region, followed by Iran where large segments of the population crave secularity, with other countries perhaps to follow in the future!?

Focusing on practical issues though, one must probe the reasons behind Israel's insistence on seeking recognition as a "Jewish State". Apart from being an excuse for stalling negotiations with the Palestinians, there are more tangible reasons for Israel's stance. They relate to Israel's expressed insistence on maintaining a dominant majority of Jewish citizens. This position precludes, or at least complicates the prospect of the return of Moslem Palestinians to occupied lands under Israeli control at present as prescribed by internationally recognized accords. This is the real sticky issue that needs to be addressed as a matter of practical priority.

Obviously, from my perspective, I prefer the prospect of a one -secular- state solution that would incorporate the Palestinian territories and put an end to apartheid in Israel. However, it seems that a one state solution is not likely to be practicable at present. So what to do then?

Being a physical planner, I believe that the borders between an Israeli and a Palestinian state could be configured to ensure their mutual security and satisfaction. The issue would be: at what financial cost?

Whatever the cost might be, I am convinced that it would be considerably less than the costs of wars that lead to loss of life and destruction, the costs of reconstruction and assistance that the world community is obliged to pay to alleviate the plight of the Palestinian people, and the generous contributions to Israel that sustain and encourage it to continue its adversarial attitudes. The world community could consider financing such a planning exercise to facilitate the realization of a two state solution.

In parallel, the international community should consider options to deal with Israel's right-wing politicians' intransigence in order to diffuse long standing problems in the Middle East which continue to threaten international security and stability.

Chapter 3

IMPERIALISM AND THE USA'S CULPABILITY AND POTENTIAL ACTION

Generally, as confirmed historically, the goal of any imperial power is to usurp the resources of other peoples to the benefit of its leaders; some benefits may trickle down to the 'imperial' common citizens. The strategy in pursuit of the goal is to build up military power in order to either invade, or otherwise be in a position to influence developments in targeted countries to the advantage of the imperial elite; the Egyptian pharos were some of the first imperialists who applied this strategy! Also, one of the main tactics of imperialism is to weaken the targeted nations by encouraging and reinforcing rifts between them, and by inciting conflicts among any existing factions of the populace. This tactic is referred to as "divide and conquer" and then "divide and rule".

The fact that a substantial portion of the world's oil and gas reserves lies beneath the soils of several Arab counties had the most to do with imperial action in the Middle East in recent decades. World wars and economic growth considerations in the West confirmed the significance of energy resources, and the advantages of gaining control over such resources. Thus, one conspiracy theory -which I ascribe to- maintains that Imperial Powers contrived to assault the ME region and to keep it in a state of 'controlled tension'. In addition to exerting influence on individual countries, creating tensions in the ME would tend to weaken the countries of the region and divert their attention to 'putting out fires' instead of 'putting their act together' to develop their own natural and human resources to their benefit.

The British were modern masters of the imperial approach as can be discerned from their actions globally, as well as in the Middle East. Their negative influence on current conditions in the ME started after the end of WW I. Having defeated the Ottoman Empire with the help of the Arabs, the British in complicity with the French divided their spoils in the Middle East into incongruous internally divided territories that they contrived to preside over.

As mentioned earlier, Britain had a mandate from the League of Nations to administer Palestine and Transjordan which led, through a series of devious moves to the emergence of the State of Israel. The British initiated the tactic of 'divide and conquer' by slicing up the area under their influence into several countries. Not only did they do that, they helped in the creation of a new adversarial entity, Israel, which was injected amidst the countries they carved out in the region. Zionism was ideally suited to cooperate with Western Powers in keeping the region in perpetual turmoil.

The British, through the Balfour declaration, indicated to Zionist leaders that the British government: "view with favour the establishment in Palestine of a national home for the Jewish people". It is noteworthy that in 1290 King Edward I issued an "Edict of Expulsion" to oust "all Jews" from England, and that England had a long history of anti-Semitism. Perhaps the English meant to make up for their misdeeds; alas at the expense of others. Although Balfour stated "it being clearly understood that nothing shall be done which may prejudice the civil and religious rights of existing non-Jewish communities in Palestine", we now know what actually transpired.

I recounted British interference with developments in Egypt. Let us consider the case of Iran. Like Egypt, it has a long and illustrious history. Unlike Egypt though, Iran has substantial oil resources. More recently, it too had a constitutional Monarchy which lasted from 1906 until 1997. It is perhaps noteworthy that the last Shah of Iran, the late Reza Pahlavi, married the sister of Egypt's King Farouk.

The Russians and the British occupied chunks of Iranian lands until 1911, and 1921 respectively. In 1921 the Prime Minister of Iran Reza Khan overthrew the ruling Qajar Dynasty, and became Shah of Iran.

When Germany invaded the USSR in 1941, the Iranians had just completed the Trans-Iranian Railway. The British and the Russians invaded Iran once again to establish a 'Persian corridor' using the railroad as a supply route to deliver Allied help from the Persian Gulf -also known as the Arabian Gulf- to the USSR. The occupation lasted until 1946. During the occupation, the British banished Shah Reza Khan and replaced him with his son Mohammad Reza Pahlavi who promised to be more cooperative with them.

In 1951 Mohammad Mosaddegh was elected prime minister of Iran. He nationalized Iran's petroleum industry; a move similar to President Nasser's nationalization of the Suez Canal which incurred Western wrath. The US and the UK cooperated in a covert operation to organize a coup d'état that deposed Mosaddegh in 1953.

Reza Pahlavi remained in power as the Shah of Iran. However, he reverted to unsavory methods to hang on to power. He banished Mosaddegh, to earn the sympathy and support of Western Powers, and relied on his secret police to rule the country with an iron fist. Demonstrations against the rule of the Shah erupted in January 1978 and continued until he fled the country a year later in

January1979. It is noteworthy that the US and the UK who helped in bringing Pahlavi to power, were reluctant to grant him asylum. President Sadat of Egypt did, and Pahlavi died in exile in Egypt shortly after his ouster.

The renowned Shia cleric Ayatollah Ruhollah Khomeini had been critical of the Shah and was living in exile abroad. He promptly returned in April 1979. Upon his return, he succeeded in arranging a national referendum which led to Iran officially becoming an Islamic Republic in 1980. The adopted constitution of Iran has been described as a hybrid of theocratic and democratic principles. While it mandates popular elections for the presidency and the parliament, it subordinates all civic entities to the guidance of a 'Guardian Council' of 13 Shia Moslem clerics and Quran experts, and a 'Supreme Leader', a 'Grand Ayatollah', as the highest authority in running the affairs of the country; the 'Grand Ayatollah' names his successor. Thus, the British and the Americans were instrumental in creating the conditions that led to the emergence of the Islamic Republic of Iran, and are culpable for any perceived negative conditions that ensued from this significant event.

No doubt that the British contributed to the evolution of negative developments in the Middle East. Among other major developments such as being involved in splitting Pakistan from India, they helped in the creation of the State of Israel, and the emergence of a Theocratic Republic in Iran, an entity which is deeply involved in the current crisis, and which is extremely critical of "the Zionist entity".

It is to be noted that the UK and France are slowly coming around to recognize their misdeeds in the ME region, and are beginning to assume a more prudent posture towards Iran and the Israeli/ Palestinian conflict.

After WW II, and the demise of the British Empire, the USA emerged as a super international power. For a few decades it competed with the USSR over control of international territories, including the ME region. After the collapse of the USSR, the US became the one and only Global Power. Israeli leaders having anticipated such potential developments courted the USA, and nurtured their relationships with it.

Initially, the US was upright in its dealings in the ME. President Eisenhower was not an imperial capitalist; he warned about 'the machinations of the military industrial complex'. As such, he interfered to halt the military attack on the Suez Canal by the British, French, and Israelis in 1956. However, consecutive US administrations, with a brief interruption during the Carter administration, progressively augmented their support of Israel. This came about as a result of American Jewish supporters of Israel, such as the American Israel Public Affairs Committee (AIPAC), who exerted ever more pressure on American politicians to influence the formulation of US policies towards Israel. The growth of their influence was briefly interrupted when President Carter orchestrated the peace agreement between Egypt and Israel.

One pertinent example of the US's stance relates to Israel's development of its nuclear arsenal, estimated to be at least 200 weapons. Although the US government may not have had an active overt role in this respect, it turned a blind eye to Israel's nuclear project which was unofficially aided by American private entities. The French were more complicit. During their occupation of Algeria, they allowed Israel to test a nuclear bomb in the Algerian desert. It behooves us to compare these conditions with the West's stance regarding Iran's nuclear ambitions.

Another example of the US's support of Israel is perhaps more intriguing. Egypt's assault on the Israeli occupying forces of the Sinai in1973 overwhelmed the Israeli military. They asked for, and got American help. US tanks ready for combat, and other war material were airlifted and applied in the battle with Egypt. This helped in reversing the tide. The Israeli army was then able to penetrate the Sinai, and the Egyptian forces retreated back to the Western banks of the Suez Canal. A cease fire agreement was reached, and ultimately a Peace Agreement was signed at Camp David under the auspices of President Carter.

The war occurred during the Nixon administration. President Nixon was not particularly supportive of Israel; it was alleged that some of the famous recorded tapes of his conversations in the White House included derogatory remarks about the Jewish people. One wonders therefore, how did he so readily come to the aid of Israel? Some have surmised that Israel might have threatened to use its nuclear weapons, and that Nixon obliged them perhaps reluctantly, to avert disastrous consequences. Some ponder further that Nixon's possible initial procrastination might have contributed to his impeachment. These presumptions could explain the fact that one of Nixon's last acts as President was to visit Egypt and promise President Sadat that the US would help Egypt in building a nuclear reactor.

Over the years as conflicts continued to rage between Israel and the Palestinians, and as Israel persisted in unlawfully building ever more Jewish settlements on occupied Palestinian lands, issues were debated by the world community at the UN. Time and time again, resolutions condemning Israel by all except the US were blocked through the US's veto power; an unparalleled record of over 50 vetoes to date. Again, compare this with the outrage regarding the Russian and Chinese exercising their veto over recent UN resolutions concerning Syria.

The above review of events illustrates how the US's support of Israel evolved from being somewhat timid and covert, to being overt and audacious. This resulted in further radicalization of Moslems and the expansion of the sentiments about their 'enemy' to include the USA. Subsequent developments further aggravated the feelings of animosity towards the USA.

In the 1980s the US supported and used the Taliban mujahedeen to oust the Russians from Afghanistan. Al Qaeda and its leader Osama Bin Laden were involved in the ouster of the Russians. After 9/11, the US invaded Afghanistan, in pursuit of Al Qaeda and Bin Laden; some maintain also for reasons relating to control of the transport of oil through Afghanistan and other US perceived strategic advantages. Ultimately, US policies turned the radical Moslem Taliban from allies to enemies.

America post-USSR evolved to progressively reflect the posture of an empire, and soon became the Global Capitalist Empire. Lord Acton said that: "absolute power corrupts absolutely". Some powerful American financiers and company CEO's, and some Israeli leaders were bent on taking advantage of the situation. Known as "neo-conservatives", their efforts climaxed and their aspirations were fulfilled during two consecutive administrations under President George W. Bush.

According to his first Secretary of the Treasury, and a former top security advisor, the first move of President GW Bush was to beat the drums of war against Iraq. I will not get into citing the grounds presented to justify a 'preemptive strike' on Iraq; it is now a matter of record that they were fabricated and false.

In my view, the US had other ulterior motives. Some related to controlling Iraq's petroleum wealth; these were not realized. Another motive was to use up US stock piles of weapons that would have to be replenished though manufacture in the US to the benefit of those who have a stake in selling weapons; the war was extremely successful in achieving that. Also, large construction companies had an eye on 'rebuilding' Iraq, after destroying it. This also was achieved to some extent through usurping Iraq's resources in devious ways, without achieving any meaningful 'rebuilding'. One noteworthy incident in this context was 'losing' 12 billion Dollars that were sent from the US to Iraq but cannot be accounted for to date as admitted by the US Government.

Shortly after the invasion, the US appointed Paul Bremer to rule Iraq. He proceeded to systematically dismantle key Sunni Baath Party political and military institutions in the country, and helped in installing Nouri Al-Maleki a Shia Moslem as Prime Minister. Al-Maleki, with Iran's backing, abused the Iraqi Sunni Moslem community for several years until he resigned his position recently under US pressure. ISIS is comprised of disgruntled Sunni Moslems including members of the dismantled Iraqi army forces. In a recent interview with Al-Arabiya TV network, Bremer seemed to relegate some of the blame for his actions on the CIA. Irrespective, the moral is that US action in Iraq led to ominous negative consequences, including the death and displacement of millions of Iraqis, overwhelming destruction, and the emergence and success of ISIS and various other splinter groups bent on terrorist attacks both in the ME and the West.

It must be noted that a number of prominent Jewish Americans vehemently promoted the invasion of Iraq. Some had visited Israel and spent weeks discussing the possibility with Israeli officials shortly before President G. W. Bush assumed power. Thus, it is no secret that Israel encouraged the assault on Iraq, and was intent on encouraging the US to attack Iran next. In fact, some critics in the US accused Israel of pushing the US into fighting Israel's wars.

It took a few years for the true reasons, and the consequences of the invasion of Iraq to surface and to sink into the consciousness of peoples around the world. This added fuel to fire further polarizing and radicalizing Moslems, and leading to more disdain of both the USA and Israel.

Before leaving this subject, it is noted that conditions have changed in the past few years. For example, the Libyans who revolted against Gaddafi asked for and received support from Western Powers including the USA. The verdict on the outcome of the ouster of Gaddafi is still unsettled, with radical Islamists running amok in the country today. Also, the Syrian 'rebels' have been seeking intervention by Western Powers in their support. The Iraqis are seeking international assistance in fighting ISIS, and the US is orchestrating international efforts in this regard. All these developments reflect radical deviation from 'business as usual' in the ME region.

Conclusion

As established above, British, French, and US Imperialism bear a heavy responsibility in bringing about the current crisis through their action in the ME region over the past several decades; including, in particular, the creation, support, and nuclear empowerment of the State of Israel.

In his speech at the UN in September 2013, President Obama stated that many nations tend to blame the USA for their predicament, but that their accusations are unwarranted. He iterated his position in his address to the UN in September 2014.

Although there is ample solid evidence that the deep roots of problems in the ME relate in great measure to the action of Western imperial forces including the USA in the past, the President's statements are true in respect of recent developments over the past few years. Western Powers have changed their attitudes, and are no longer the main instigators of problems in the region. The question thus arises as to what they could possibly do next to address the current crisis?

To begin with, since the Israeli- Palestinian issue has been long identified as lying at the roots of problems in the region, Western Powers could do what they can to address this issue. As mentioned earlier, the English and French have addressed the issue by taking some steps towards recognition of a Palestinian state. The burden of such efforts though lies with the USA, since it is the main supporter of Israel.

The Arab and Moslem peoples of the region have been counting on the USA to exercise its influence over Israel to defuse tensions, especially those arising from the expansion of unlawful Israeli settlements on Palestinian lands, by convincing Israel to halt these activities. This would have facilitated negotiations between Israel and the Palestinians, and to the relaxation of tensions in the region. The Obama administration did attempt to do that on several occasions, but was met by Israeli defiance and humiliation of the envoys that carried the US's pleas to Israel; including Vice President Biden and Foreign Secretary Kerry. No wonder that President Obama and Prime Minister Netanyahu do not seem to get along well with each other. The fact though, is that the US is not in a position to exercise political pressure on Israel; the opposite is true!

Israel is the only nation in the world that is in a position to influence political developments in the USA. This is evident in the attitude and action of the Congress of the USA which is flagrantly and embarrassingly pro Israel. As mentioned previously, this is due to the activities of the super powerful Jewish/Israeli lobby in the USA over several decades, which does not seem to be wavering. Accordingly, one can no longer count on the US to intervene with Israeli action; unless the Jewish community in the USA allows this to happen. The recent US action in the UN to block the Palestinian initiative to involve the international community in addressing the Palestinian gripe with Israel, and the more recent invitation of PM Netanyahu by Congressman Boehner to address a joint session of the US Congress in defiance of President Obama, confirm the extent of the influence of Israel on political developments in the USA.

Bottom line: Western Powers including the USA have not been able to alter Israel's stance in the region. In light of PM Netanyahu's recent action, they might consider imposing sanctions on Israel to sway Israel to abandon its intransigent attitudes. They could also support Fatah's efforts to mobilize the international community and the UN to address the Palestinian people's plight.

Otherwise, what else could one expect Western Powers to do in the way of addressing the current crisis?

The present US administration under President Obama inherited serious problems initiated by the previous administration of President G. W. Bush. Paramount among these problems was internal dire economic conditions. Addressing those entailed curtailing US military expenditures which contributed to recent US deficits and other economic woes, by spending trillions of Dollars on foreign military ventures. This explains President Obama's draw down of troops from abroad, and his reluctance to send boots on the ground to troubled areas around the globe; preferring to rely on drones and special operations instead. Thus, the Obama administration was reluctant and slow in reacting to the recent flaring up of conflicts in Syria and Iraq. Only when conditions appeared to be getting completely out of control in Iraq, did the President reluctantly allow air strikes and sending a limited number of 'advisors' to the most troubled areas. He is doing that in collaboration with both Western and local Arab allies, including Saudi Arabia, the UAE, and Jordan.

The President's action seems to be generally appreciated by several countries in the region for the time being. However, current allied nations' action is not expected to defuse the crisis any time soon. The US could consider more vigorous concerted action in support of allied Arab efforts, without direct intervention by its own military forces.

At least the Obama administration has refrained from the kinds of blatant intrusions practiced by the preceding administration of President G. W. Bush. Instead, the current American method is more covert and nuanced. It is reflected in its efforts to negotiate with Iran over nuclear issues. The US administration is urged to continue to apply this approach; irrespective of PM Netanyahu's disapproval, which he clearly expressed in his address to the joint session of Congress on March 3, 2015!

Although the current US administration is conducting its foreign policy in the ME in more prudent ways compared with the preceding administration of President G W Bush, the administration's recent posture towards Egypt is incomprehensible! I feel that way because Egypt, a major power in the region that is deeply involved in containing the rise of Islamism, seems to be snubbed by the Obama administration.

At present, radical Islamists are the main perpetrators of strife, violence, and terrorism in Egypt as well as in many other Middle Eastern countries. Irrespective of whom to blame for the initiation and proliferation of radical Islamism, reversing the growing tide of this trend must be appreciated and prized. This is exactly what the revolution of June 30 which was consummated on the 3rd of July, 2013 achieved and which the current Egyptian government has been attempting to consolidate. Therefore, I was and remain quite baffled by the US's stance towards the second Egyptian revolution and the current government!

Some maintain that the US assisted the MB to ascend to power. Perhaps not fully cognizant of the fundamental nature of the MB and its long term goals and objectives, the Obama Administration felt that the MB were likely to win the elections and started dealing with the MB in an attempt to be in a position to influence future developments.

It is also alleged that the US concluded certain deals with the MB. The answer to the question "what deals were concluded?" depends on whom you ask. Totally contradictory views have been asserted by opposing factions in Egyptian society. The reason is that different factions assess conditions from their respective points of view, which are often diametrically opposed. The result is that the US was being inconsistently accused of perceived contradictory action. This is evidence of the general mood that prevails in Egypt as well as in other ME countries which emerged as a consequence of historical precedents, namely: any perceived negative developments whatsoever must be ascribed to the interference of the USA and/or Israel. If deals were made, I have wondered, to what particular ends!? And, in the first place, how could the US have felt comfortable in dealing with the MB!?

When the issue of control over the Nile waters by countries upstream arose, some MB leader said: not to worry, we shall pray and God will help us in resolving this issue. Some others said: by God's will we shall defeat the Zionist enemy and soon have control over Jerusalem. The opera house in Cairo was closed and its director fired during President Morsi's tenure. These statements and acts reflect the true colors of the MB, and lead me to raise the question: what if the MB were allowed to remain in power as many critics in the West suggested? Since ousting the MB is a relatively recent development, and since I have more knowledge of developments in Egypt compared with other countries I will venture to answer this question.

Some critics of 'the coup' say that had the opponents of the Islamist regime waited for three years until the next elections were to be held, they could have used the time to organize and perhaps win the next elections in democratic fashion. This seems to me to be unrealistic, because the MB was taking every possible step to prevent such an eventuality. They were appointing MB operatives in key positions in all branches of government; from governors all the way to school teachers and policemen. Thus, judging from their action during one year in power, a more reasonable expectation would be that they could have maintained power for generations to come.

MB sympathetic entities came to power earlier in Tunisia and Libya, and a Sunni Caliphate was in the budding. Its population would have been subjected to live under conditions similar to those that evolved in Iran, which have prevailed there for several decades. This would have entailed slim prospects for the return of secularity to the region; a most undesirable outcome from my considered position.

After the fact of the MB's initial success, it was understandable that the US which holds itself as a champion of democracy, felt bound to accept the results of the national election that brought the MB to power, and later on to object to the ouster of President Morsi. Many in the West held this position. They still refer to the new government as a military junta that deposed an elected government, a no-no in democratic annals. However, others view developments as reflecting a popular uprising which was supported by the military to arrest and reverse dangerous and unacceptable developments.

As it were, the US's initial reaction to the second Egyptian revolution of 2013 was to renege on payment of about one billion Dollars in financial aid to Egypt as prescribed in the Peace Accords with Israel, and to criticize the revolution. Also, the Egyptian government seems to have requested military supplies from the US which the US refused to provide. This led the Egyptian government to seek assistance from Russia.

For a while, tensions between the USA and Egypt seemed to be easing off. However, most recent developments indicate that this détente may not have lasted for long.

In February 2015 the Obama administration welcomed an MB delegation from different ME countries in Washington, and President Vladimir Putin visited Cairo and agreed that Russia will help Egypt in achieving its economic goals, and promised to assist in the construction of two nuclear reactors!? All of this is reminiscent of the historic developments of the relations between the USA and Egypt in conjunction with the construction of the Aswan High Dam; with potentially similar international ramification.

The moral thus is that the US could have treaded more carefully and deliberately in its dealings with Egypt. I do not have insider information about what goes on behind the scenes. However, it seems to me that serious avenues of cooperation with Egypt to address the current crisis in the ME could have been explored, agreed to, and implemented. Conditions though could have evolved in certain directions that might preclude such potential collaboration.

Egypt now is approaching the UN to support an international force to combat radical terrorist Islamists, and in parallel, is working with Saudi Arabia and other sympathetic Arab countries to form a strike force to achieve the same end; without specifically requesting the USA to participate.

Frankly, I am rather pleased about this turn of events, for several reasons.

The US contributed in profound ways to the emergence of problems in the ME, and is not likely to be ever fully trusted in dealing with the problems it created. Therefore, after inflicting so much damage, and incurring the wrath of Arab and Moslem populations, the USA should consider withdrawing from proactive involvement in the region, and letting the natives address current problems on their own. Instead of leading and dictating courses for action, it is advised to stand by and provide assistance if requested. This would be to the US's advantage through savings on the expenditure of both moral and financial capital.

On the other hand, Egypt is both a creditable and capable entity that is fully qualified to address the current crisis. Egypt itself is suffering from the 'machinations' of radical Islamism and has a legitimate gripe that it wishes to settle with radical Islamists. Also, the Egyptian army which is highly ranked by virtue of its competence and combat readiness is quite capable of carrying out necessary military action to combat radical Islamist forces, compared with the other Arab armies which the US is currently supporting in the region. In addition, Egypt earned the trust and support of prominent Arab countries including Saudi Arabia, the UAE, and Kuwait. The US could recognize and support the leadership position of these countries in the region.

Generally, the US needs to continue President Obama's approach of avoiding confrontation, exploring avenues of cooperation and economic assistance, and addressing issues through diplomacy. Hopefully the next Republican controlled Congress will be prudent enough to follow suit!

Oddly enough though, prominent Republican politicians who do not agree with President Obama's general approach, have recently expressed views in support of the second Egyptian revolution and President El Sisi!!

Chapter 4

THE CULPABILITY AND POTENTIAL ACTION OF ARAB LEADERS

For decades, many held the view that the resolution of the Israeli-Palestinian problem would lead to stable conditions and normalized relations among the nations of the ME; I felt this way myself. Resolving the problem lied mainly with the Israelis, the Palestinians, and the United States; sadly to no avail. Now, although resolving the Israeli-Palestinian issue would constitute a momentous step towards addressing the problems of the region, resolving the Israeli-Palestinian problem alone is not likely to bring an end to the current crisis; or rather, the numerous crises manifested in several countries in the region.

In my view, the last imperial act of invading and occupying Iraq, which Israel encouraged the US and its allies to carry out, radically altered conditions in the region in ways that directly contributed to flaring the current crisis, and at the same time, precluded any clear-cut solutions to addressing the problems of the region. Alas, Western Powers sought a state of 'controlled tension' in the region which evolved through their action jointly with Israel into a state of 'uncontrollable chaos'.

The raging chaos at present is being perpetrated essentially by numerous native Islamist entities, and sensible action by these diverse entities is prerequisite to ending the current crisis; a complex and difficult proposition to accomplish.

Although I follow the news of developments in the ME from different sources both in Arabic and English on a daily basis, it is becoming difficult for me to form a clear view of who is fighting whom in many areas, and the true aims of various warring factions and their supporters. The complexity of developments is evident in Iraq, Syria, Libya, and Yemen where conditions are extremely muddled. Developments in Gaza and Hamas's relations with Fatah and Egypt are also challenging. Thus, finding solutions to prevailing problems seems to be getting more complicated as the ME crisis continues to unfold. Conditions could get even worse, and may not get better for years to come!

Furthermore, developments on the ground are changing quite rapidly, and depend on the outcome of key events; for example Al Maleki's decision to step down as prime minister of Iraq as he did, the results of elections in Tunisia which are now known to have favored secularists, and developments involving warring factions in Yemen which are changing in significant ways from one day to the other. Also, a terrorist act here or there could have far reaching consequences; such as recent terrorist incidents in Egypt. The equations that one is attempting to address are constantly changing and thus defying solution. In spite of the complexity of problems though, two observations are both obvious and relevant:

First: the only beneficiary of the current turmoil appears to be Israel; I cannot think of anyone else since no ME country appears to delight in observing the carnage that is unfolding in the region, and since Western Powers seem to be acting to contain the crisis before it spills over into ever more acts of Islamist terrorism in Western countries. Prominent Israelis on the other hand have often expressed the view: let the Arabs kill each other, and let us move on with our agenda; a Greater Larger Israel. The Israeli government is taking advantage of the moment by unlawfully authorizing the construction of over 1,000 dwelling units on occupied Palestinian territories!

Second: the main losers in the current turmoil are the warring tribal and radical Islamists themselves since large numbers of them are getting killed on a daily basis, together with millions of the local populations that are being massacred or forced to flee their homes due to the flaring conflicts. In addition, recent conflicts led to massive destruction of property and infrastructure in many Arab countries. It will take many years and billions of Dollars to restore the damage that resulted from the Islamists' ill-advised action over the past few years.

I cannot help but crying out loud to all the tribal Islamist warring factions and their leaders and supporters: "Shame on you, you have fallen in the trap of 'divide and rule' that was set up for you by others".

Having made this proclamation and gotten it out of my system, I would like to classify issues into two main categories: 'old' and 'new'.

We have the 'old' interconnected problems of Israel and Imperialism which have persisted for decades and were addressed in the previous chapters 2 and 3. We also have certain 'old' problems relating to Moslem populations and their leaders, of which examples in the case of Egypt were discussed in chapter 1. Then there are relatively 'new' issues that I consider to have resulted from the persistence of the three categories of 'old' problems. They are manifested in the current crisis and relate predominantly to Moslem populations and their leaders.

This chapter addresses both the 'old' and the 'new' issues relating to Moslem populations and their leaders. Certain observations and views relating to the Arab Spring and to its role in the emergence of the current crisis are pertinent.

The current crisis relates mainly to the action of Islamist factions in the region. Now, Islamism resulted from the action of imperial powers in collaboration with Israel, and was lurking in the region as reflected in the presence of Al Qaeda and other similar entities in several countries of the ME way before the Arab Spring took off. The Arab Spring reflects an uprising of native populations against their leaders for legitimate and understandable reasons. It already brought about positive conditions in Tunisia, and promises to lead to further positive developments in the region. The Arab Spring did not 'cause' current problems; it simply encouraged the release of bent up pressures that were building up in the region for decades.

Alas, misguided Islamists immediately embarked on taking advantage of the vacuum that resulted from the ouster of several national leaders to establish and spread Islamist rule in the region. This, in turn, heightened tensions between Sunni and Shia entities that were historically vying for power in the region.

Thus, I designate the 'old' category of problems as 'pre Iraq war and Arab Spring', and the 'new' problems that are reflected in the current crisis as 'post Iraq war and Arab Spring'.

Notable among the political leaders whose actions reflect the 'old' leadership issues in the region is Saddam Hussein. A Sunni Moslem, Saddam ruled the predominantly Shia Moslem population of Iraq for decades. He was supported by several consecutive US administrations. They encouraged, and supported him to wage war on Iran. The war started in 1980 shortly after the Iranian revolution that brought a theocratic Shia government to power in Iran. The war continued until 1988. It started presumably over border disputes between the two countries. Eight years of military conflict did not result in any modification of these borders. Instead, it resulted in 500,000 Iraqis and Iranians killed and many more injured, in addition to sapping the resources of both countries.

It must be noted that Saddam Hussein used chemical weapons in the war with Iran, as well as on Iraqi Kurdish dissidents in his own country, with scant reprimand from Western Powers. It has been reported that US officials knew of Saddam's use of chemical weapons and provided Iraq with satellite imagery to guide strikes against Iranian troop concentrations. Compare the US's stance vis-à-vis Saddam at that time, with the rhetoric used to drum up support for invading Iraq, and the recent uproar regarding the Syrian regime's alleged use of chemical weapons. This illustrates the US's earlier posture towards Iraq! However, Saddam was also an outspoken opponent of Israel. At some point he attacked Israel with Scud missiles thus incurring Israel's wrath; and by consequence the US's.

In August 1990, Iraq invaded and occupied its neighbor to the south Kuwait; some claim that the US had a hand in Saddam thinking that he could get away with that. The US under then president Bush senior mounted Desert Storm and ousted Iraq out of Kuwait. Saddam's venture led to a massacre of his army, and substantial financial losses to both the Kuwaiti and Iraqi people.

On March 20, 2003 the US administration orchestrated the invasion of Iraq by a coalition of countries on the false pretext that Iraq possessed weapons of mass destruction. The invasion was carried out for other reasons as discussed earlier in this book. The toll amounted to over 600,000 Iraqi people killed, 5,000 US soldiers killed and tens of thousands maimed for life on both sides. Millions of Iraqis were uprooted and displaced. Iraq's infrastructure was also substantially degraded. Saddam Hussein, went into hiding, was found, tried, and hanged in December 2006. Iraq has not yet recovered from the destruction inflicted by the US allied invasion.

For some time during Saddam's rule, Iraq enjoyed relative internal stability and economic prosperity, though at a great cost of human rights abuses; it is reported that Saddam on occasion pulled his gun and shot some of his opponents dead. On the whole, Saddam Hussein's contribution to developments in Iraq and the ME in general ultimately proved to be disastrous. His actions exemplify the negative contribution of some ME political leaders to the evolution of negative conditions both in his own country as well as the ME region.

Another national leader whose actions reflect the 'old' problems of political leadership in the ME is Muammar Al- Gaddafi of Libya. He was by all accounts an eccentric figure who created unconventional political and civic structures that he relied upon to rule the country for 42 years. Although he was not as ruthless as Saddam in running internal affairs, he squandered significant financial resources on external foreign ventures in Africa and elsewhere. He too was an avid critic of Israel, and often held a confrontational attitude towards the USA.

Libya was implicated in several terrorist acts abroad including the downing of Pan Am flight 103 over Lockerbie, Scotland. His actions led to the imposition of UN sanctions on Libya in 1992. By 2009 though, he managed to mend his fences with the West; business prospects were involved in appeasing his main adversaries the USA and the UK.

As in the case of Saddam in Iraq, Libya enjoyed relative internal stability and economic prosperity under the rule of Gaddafi. At least he kept Libyan tribes from warring against each other. However, although the Libyans were reasonably prosperous, there was relatively little they could do in their own country to enjoy their prosperity. I got a flavor of conditions in Libya when I visited Tripoli in 1991on a UN mission.

My assignment was to assess a proposed government program to privatize the housing sector. Housing at the time was built, maintained, and managed by the Ministry of Housing. A meeting was arranged with the Minister, and a senior official was assigned as my liaison. I asked for, and was provided with numerous planning studies and relevant material for my study. Shortly thereafter however, I discovered that Gaddafi had previously abolished all forms of private ownership. The issue thus turned out not to be a technical urban planning problem, but rather a fundamental question as to how to privatize housing in the total absence of privately owned land and building properties!?

I flew to Tripoli from New York with a stopover in Vienna. The only Western airlines that flew to Tripoli then were Austrian Airlines and Luft Hanza, since both Austria and Germany continued to have oil interests in Libya. I did not stay overnight in Vienna as I had wished to, because the UN wanted to rush me to Tripoli before the contemplated imposition of sanctions. It took me five weeks in Tripoli poring over the documents I was given, and completing my report to the UN. They turned to be the most miserable five weeks of my life.

Expatriates residing in Tripoli lived in exclusive gated compounds, I understand, with excellent amenities. Poor me, although I had a reasonable room in the second best hotel in town, I had to contend with the limited choice of mediocre meals that were available in the hotel, and TV programs that featured only religious programs and local news covering Gaddafi speeches and demonstrations by his supporters; he was trying to display to 'the world' his popularity in the country in an attempt to avert UN sanctions! Sometimes I ventured out of the hotel to find a respectable restaurant where I could order a decent meal, or a grocery store where I could buy something that enjoy eating, but couldn't find any. Perhaps I did not know the town well enough! Perhaps nobody wanted to show me a good time because of my affiliation with the UN, which was derided in Libya at the time!?

I was under pressure to complete my assignment in four weeks -it took me reluctantly five- and had little time for entertainment anyway. However, I needed some exercise to keep my sanity; in anticipation I carried my tennis racket in my luggage. I had to take a taxi ride that seemed to last forever to the outskirts of Tripoli to get to the nearest club with tennis courts. Later, I learned that Gaddafi was discouraging all kinds of 'bourgeois' sports, which in his definition included m most practiced in the West. He only encouraged marathon running, where 'the people' at large were urged to participate in regular marathon events organized by the government around the country!

On my trip back to the USA, I did stay overnight in Vienna. I can hardly find the words to describe my elation to being there, and the extent of the contrast that I felt between conditions in Tripoli and Vienna. No wonder in my mind about why the Libyans took the opportunity of the Arab Spring to rebel against the rule of Gaddafi!

More seriously, Gaddafi could be blamed for depriving the Libyans of civic structures that could have continued to function after his demise. He is definitely one of the political leaders that could be blamed for the evolution of negative conditions both in Libya and the ME.

Bin Ali of Tunisia is yet another member of the 'old' guard of leaders who affected conditions in negative ways. However, his contribution to 'old' problems was largely limited to Tunisia with little impact on neighboring countries.

Saddam, Gaddafi, and Bin Ali are leaders whose action exemplifies past political leadership problems in Arab countries. Following are examples of lingering and current leadership problems in relevant countries involved in the present crisis, starting with those suffering the most damage from the prevailing carnage in the region.

Iraq experienced the most devastation of any country in the ME in recent history. The US allied invasion in addition to inflicting substantial damage, also led to the initiation and continuation of serious internal upheavals in the country.

Saddam Hussein's contribution to the woes of Iraq was covered above. Recent Iraqi political leaders contributed to the emergence of the 'new' category of problems in Iraq. Notable among those leaders is Nori Al Malki, a Shia Moslem whom the US helped in installing as Prime Minister after invading Iraq. He is one Iraqi political leader who unquestionably contributed to the emergence of the current crisis. During his tenure, he systematically abused the Iraqi Sunni minority, thus directly leading to the emergence and subsequent success of the Sunni ISIS. Recent accusations that 50,000 Shia Iraqis were receiving wages as members of the army without actually serving as such confirm allegations of his corruption and mismanagement. Thankfully he recently agreed to step down as Prime Minister.

The new political leadership in Iraq is struggling to cope with seemingly insurmountable problems, including a deeply divided population, and the presence of local and foreign radical Islamist forces which are ravaging the country. The new leadership is doing what it can to cope, with relatively limited outside support. At present, the Iraqi government is trying to regain some of the Iraqi territories lost to ISIS, and the US is standing by to assess the results of the government's military action, and to establish how the Iraqis will manage on their own. It remains to be seen how the government's efforts will play out. At any rate, there are no clear indications signaling an end to the raging conflicts in Iraq.

Syria, ruled by the Al-Assad family for decades, is another prominent example reflecting the prevailing carnage in the ME. The current president Basshar Al-Assad 'inherited' the presidency of Syria from his father Hafez Al-Assad. Both father and son must be included as ME leaders whose actions led to the flaring and persistence of the current crisis; thus contributing to both the 'old' and the 'new' categories of problems in the region. I am inclined to more readily ascribe culpability to the son rather than to his father, in particular, due to Basshar's momentous contribution to the emergence of 'new' and continuing problems.

The family belongs to a minority of Shia Alawites that ruled the Syrian majority of Sunni Moslem since 1970. Bashar Al-Assad and his father are old foes of Israel; Israel occupied the Syrian Golan Heights in the 1967 war, and when Israel invaded Lebanon in 1982, it also attacked Syria. I suspect that Syria's adversarial attitude towards Israel and the fact that Syria possessed chemical weapons that could have been used against Israel must have influenced recent developments in Syria.

In March 2011, the Syrian Sunni majority inspired by the Arab Spring, revolted against the rule of the minority Alawite government of Bashar Al-Assad and initiated a civil war that continues to rage at present. The toll to date is over 200,000 killed, several hundred thousand injured, nearly 4 million refugees to neighboring countries, and roughly 6 million Syrians displaced internally. The rebel forces who oppose the Al-Assad government are comprised of several Sunni Moslem groups, including members of Al Qaeda, ISIS, and other less radical groups of local dissidents. It is noteworthy that the Shia cleric Hasan Nasrallah who heads the Hezb Ullah party in Lebanon, with the urging and support of Iran, is sending thousands of Shia fighters into Syria to support Al-Assad.

Basshar Al-Assad systematically resists reconciliation with his opponents, and thus is partially culpable for the carnage in his own country. He is relying on the Russians and Chinese for international support; they both vetoed the adoption of UN resolutions against Syria.

In spite of several international attempts to find a negotiated political solution to the problems in Syria, there is no indication that a political solution is attainable any time soon.

The borders between Iraq and Syria are several hundred miles long. The problems in both countries are spilling over their mutual borders. The intricacies of these problems fall in the category that I admit are difficult to understand and address. They are likely to defy resolution for years to come.

Libya is another country that is suffering in profound ways from the brunt of the current crisis in the ME. The rebellion against Gaddafi led MB sympathetic politicians to assume power in Libya. However, subsequent developments in Tunisia and Egypt encouraged the Libyans to overthrow the Islamist government that took over after Gaddafi's demise. This act led to a civil war that is still raging in the country.

Gaddafi's contribution to 'old' leadership problems was covered above. The leaders of all the tribal and Islamist factions of all persuasion involved in the conflicts in Libya at present must share blame for the 'new' problems in their own country as well as other Arab nations; since Libya exports both weapons and combatants to Egypt, Palestine, Iraq, and Syria. Their action certainly reflects the 'new' category of problems that emerged in the region 'post Iraq war', which continue to plague the region.

Several attempts have been made to restore civic order in Libya, including national elections and attempts to conceive a constitution acceptable to the varied parties in the prevailing conflicts. Sadly to no avail! Also, in spite of international efforts to reach a political solution to the prevailing problems in Libya, the country's population remains severely divided, without an acknowledged national government to run its affairs. The civil war continues without an end in sight.

Yemen is the forth Arab country to suffer from continuing major upheavals 'post Iraq war'. Recent history reflects two entities in Yemen. The Yemen Arab Republic established in the North in 1962, and the People's Republic of South Yemen established in the South in 1967. The two entities were united as the Republic of Yemen in 1990. Yemen is a tribal society with a long history of conflicts between Sunni and Shia tribes vying for a fair share of the country's rich oil resources which happen to be located in the South of the country.

The most famous political leader of Yemen is Ali Abdullah Saleh. He served as President of the Yemen Arab Republic from 1978 to 1990, and as President of the Republic of Yemen upon unification of the North and South in 1990. In January, 2011, a popular uprising toppled Saleh after ruling for decades; at some point he was severely injured when the presidential palace was attacked by Yemeni rebels. More recently, Saleh allied himself with the Houthi Shia tribe, which, with Iran's help, is creating havoc in Yemen. By his action he is contributing to flaring lethal conflicts between Sunni and Shia Moslems in Yemen.

The moral is that Saleh seems to be desperately clinging on to power, irrespective of the consequences to the people of his country; it is reported that before his ouster, he was grooming his son Ahmed to take over the presidency. As such, he is not much different from the other leaders identified in this book as contributing to negative developments in the region, particularly in his case, due to his involvement in flaring the current crisis in Yemen.

At present, the Yemeni people are deeply divided and involved in a civil war, with no nationally recognized government. There are no serious indications that Yemen will return to stable conditions any time soon.

Palestinian political leaders, compared with other Arab leaders, were more directly involved in the evolution of negative developments in the region since their inception. While deeply sympathetic and appreciative of their desire to find ways to address the plight of their people, Palestinian political leaders have often miscalculated their moves. In their efforts to address their conflict with Israel, they often unintentionally contributed to the dire predicament of their people. Their action over the decades reflects examples of both the 'old' and the 'new' leadership problems in the region.

'Old' leaders, mainly the late Yasser Arafat, are culprit. For example, when the West Bank was under Jordan's control, the PLO attacked the Jordanian army in 1970. The army's forceful response led to the massacre of Palestinians in Jordan, referred to as the incident of Black September, and to the ouster of thousands of Palestinians from Jordan to Lebanon. Also, many insignificant Palestinian attacks on Israel, consistently gave Israel an excuse for retaliation with overwhelming force, and thus, brought more hurt and destruction upon the Palestinian people than on the Israelis. The current leaders of Fatah though have generally displayed more nuanced and prudent attitudes.

The most recent rocket attacks on Israel by Hamas in 2014, is a glaring example of 'new' Palestinian leadership problems. Also, Hamas's more recent alleged involvement in terrorist incidents in the Sinai does not bode well for their relations with Egypt, and thus, harm the Palestinian cause. These are but a few examples illustrating Palestinian leaders' unfortunate miscalculations.

The rift between Fatah and Hamas leaves the Palestinians divided, and will tend to prolong their suffering. However, Fatah's recent attitude and moves to address the Israeli-Palestinian conflict through appeal to the international community revives hopes for attaining some relief for the Palestinian people from the oppressive conditions imposed by Israel.

Lebanon and ***Jordan*** were deeply involved in developments in the region for decades. They also suffer from the brunt of the current crisis; in the least by bearing the burden of harboring millions of refugees from Palestine, Iraq, and Syria. However,

Lebanon and Jordan were fortunate in not having the kind of blatantly treacherous political leaders that deserve to be mentioned critically here!

On the other hand, other ME countries deserve to be mentioned. Especially countries who, while not directly suffering from the consequences of the current crisis, are nonetheless actively engaged in initiating and aggravating problems.

Iran is a most prominent example in this respect. Iran's leaders are not targeted for critique on account of their nuclear ambitions which brought about international sanctions that are hurting the Iranian people; the sanctions are not hurting other peoples in the region. However, Iran has been aggravating conflicts between Shia and Sunni Moslems in Lebanon, Syria, Iraq, and Yemen for many years through support of sundry Shia Moslem militias and entities. Also, Iranian leaders took advantage of the vacuum that ensued from the Arab Spring to relentlessly escalate their involvement in the internal affairs of other countries in the region. They are deeply involved in flaring the current crisis, and are well deserving of blame for their contribution to the creation and perpetuation of 'new' problems.

Qatar is also notable in this context. With a very small population of nationals and huge natural gas resources, it has the highest per capita income in the world. In the past, Qatar had scantly any influence on developments in region. However, its recently acquired wealth tempted its leaders to meddle in the internal affairs of other countries.

Qatar is reported to have supported and financed the rise of the MB to power in Egypt by dishing out billions of Dollars to the MB. After Mr. Morsi was elected President, Qatar loaned Egypt several billion dollars; at some point Qatar tried to secure the sole rights to develop the Giza pyramids area for tourism! Qatar reacted frantically to the ouster of President Morsi, perhaps due to losing its investment in affecting economic developments in Egypt; the Egyptian government though recently paid back the loan. Qatar is also a staunch supporter of Hamas in Gaza.

I lived in Qatar on and off for a number of years and found it difficult to understand its policies. On the one hand it hosts the Aljazeera TV network which has been consistently critical of US policies and action. On the other hand, it has the largest US military base outside the USA. So, are they with, or against the USA!?

Now, Qatar and Aljazeera continue to side with the MB and other Sunni camps. Qatar is reported to finance all sorts of Islamist Sunni entities scattered all over the ME region, thus contributing to the perpetuation of conflicts. I am not sure about Qatar's ultimate goals and objectives. Perhaps Qatar was, and is still yearning for the establishment of a Sunni Moslem Caliphate? To what ultimate end, I wonder!

I distinctly recall the brawl between Qatar and Iran over the rights to exploit the so called North Dome; a huge bubble of natural gas beneath the Arabian Gulf; or Persian Gulf, depending on whom you ask! That was over twenty years ago when I happened to live in Qatar. Qatar won the contest by invoking international law.

It is no secret that the Qatari and Iranian governments have been adversaries for quite some time. Their animosity towards each other is reflected in their recent actions, which are sadly leading to the death of thousands of nationals of *other* ME countries. To be fair though, Iran, in addition to providing financial support to Shia entities, did send a number of 'advisors' and combatants to troubled areas some of whom were killed. Qatar's contribution though is limited to paying the wages of fighters and the purchase of military gear. Qatari nationals are not engaged in the actual fighting in the region! Qatari leaders are certainly involved in, and culpable for the creation of the 'post Iraq war' problems in the region.

Turkey is also to blame for the current crisis. Like Qatar, but not to the same extent, Turkey's political leaders have been supporting Sunni factions in several countries in the ME, including Hamas in Gaza, the MB in Egypt and other splinter Sunni radical Islamists elsewhere in the region, thus contributing to the perpetuation of conflicts. Turkish political leaders also deserve blame for their attitudes and action.

Saudi Arabia, the **UAE**, and **Kuwait** also contributed to the evolution of the current crisis, mainly by keeping a blind eye to the activities of Islamists, in particular the Wahabis in their countries, and by allowing their citizens to make generous contributions to many radical Islamist entities in the region. More recently though, they recognized the dangers associated with having allowed such conditions, and started to take steps to deal with the spread of Islamism.

Political leaders are not the only leaders to be blamed for negative developments in the region. Religious leaders must share the blame.

Conflicts between Sunnis and Shiites erupted throughout Islamic history, starting shortly after Prophet Mohammed's death, and flaring up occasionally over the centuries. Sadly, many religious leaders have recently indulged in rekindling the adversarial sentiments and aggravating the rift between Sunni and Shia Moslems. They fell into the trap to 'divide and rule' alluded to above, and are certainly to be blamed for flaring the current crisis in the ME.

The influence of religious leaders is reflected in the most pervasive destructive phenomena in many countries of the ME. Over many years car bombs exploded on a regular basis in Iraq, Syria, Yemen, and Lebanon killing scores of Shia and Sunni Moslems as each faction targeted the other. Car bombs killed innocent people in Pakistan, and Afghanistan for different reasons, albeit of late less frequently. The most atrocious of such acts are being committed by ISIS on a daily basis now in Iraq; including beheadings, summary executions, whole sale massacres and uprooting of innocent people. Similar atrocities involving Sunni and Shia Moslems have been committed by warring factions in Syria for over four years. Irrespective of geographic location, radical Islamists are invariably involved in these heinous crimes.

Many religious leaders -imams and clerics- indulge in aggravating divisions between their respective Sunni and Shia Moslem congregations, and encourage and support sundry warring factions in the region. Several Sunni religious leaders affiliated with the Moslem Brotherhood, and many Shia clerics such as Hasan Nasrallah of Hezbollah in Lebanon, openly call for lethal struggle between Sunnis and Shiites. All such religious leaders must share the blame for flaring the current crisis.

Arabs and Moslems can be generally blamed for falling for the misleading rhetoric of some of their irresponsible political and religious leaders, and for tolerating radical Islamists amongst them. Sadly, these general attitudes existed 'pre Iraq war' and continue to prevail at present; albeit with more serious consequences.

Conclusion

As established above, many Arab and Moslem countries had autocratic and often brutal rulers who conducted their countries' affairs with the main goal of staying in power. Some had geopolitical aspirations and interfered in their neighbors affairs with mutually detrimental consequences. Also, many religious leaders indulged in heightening tensions between Sunni and Shia Moslems in the region.

Accordingly, the political leaders who acted in adverse ways and failed to address economic and human rights issues in a judicious manner and the religious leaders who aggravated the rift between Sunni and Shia Moslems have both contributed to the evolution of the current crisis. The people who accepted and tolerated such conditions are also culprit at least by virtue of their acquiescence.

However, it is noteworthy to compare the locals' influence on developments with that of foreign forces.

Zionism aimed to colonize Palestine, and Western Powers aimed to destabilize and usurp the regions' resources. Both interfered with local conditions often with brutal force to attain their ulterior egocentric goals. Their intent was to benefit themselves, and their action only harmed the local Arab and Moslem populations.

Local leaders on the other hand, were forced to assume a reactive mode to external pressures. While sometimes miscalculating their moves, they generally aimed at improving the lot of their people. Their actions had both negative and positive consequences.

Irrespective of the relative gravity and the respective contributions of locals and foreigners to the evolution of the current crisis, we must try to address prevailing problems.

Islamism in various forms is the most glaring symptom of the current crisis. Accordingly, the first priority for action by all involved is to attempt to diffuse prevailing Islamist sentiments and attitudes; in all fairness, we need to address religious ideologies in general, including Zionism. This being the case, I decided to dedicate the following chapter 5 to deal with this topic.

At any rate, we need to explore courses of action that could have some immediate impact on defusing the flaring conflicts.

Ideological differences relating to the understanding and application of Sharia law are involved in some conflicts, as for example in Tunisia, and Egypt. In most cases however, the current crisis reflects fierce competition over assuming political power with the aim of controlling economic resources to the benefit of one or the other of the warring factions. This is obviously the case in Iraq, Syria, Libya, and Yemen. In some cases the conflicts regarding economic matters happen to be between Sunni and Shia Moslems.

Irrespective of the reasons for conflict, it is evident that the way the Islamists involved are going about achieving their goals is proving to be counterproductive. Developments on the ground do not indicate any prospects for a clear winner in the flaring conflicts. Therefore, the various factions involved in conflict must consider alternative courses of action that could be to their mutual benefit. The clear prudent alternative is to engage in peaceful negotiation instead of terrorism and war.

Thus, one could approach the young men and women of all persuasion who are committing terrorist acts or are directly engaged in lethal conflicts, and ask them to cease and desist from involvement in the conflicts instigated by their often deceitful leaders. True, some are fighting for the privilege to participate in running their country's affairs, and thus to secure a fair share of its resources. However, one could point out that the issues they are fighting about are not amenable to resolution through terrorist acts and armed struggle. The issues involved are more amenable to resolution through peaceful negotiation. Therefore, they are unnecessarily sacrificing their lives.

Getting this message to those involved though, is problematic. Whether the young men and women would be inclined to listen is even more questionable. Therefore, by necessity, we have to rely on political and religious leaders to alter their ways, and for them to reach out to their respective followers to effect meaningful change.

One measure by political leaders that could have immediate results would be to deprive warring factions of the flow of funds and war material that sustain their activities. Saudi Arabia, the UAE, Kuwait, and Bahrain have taken steps in this direction by clamping down on individuals and local entities that provide financial support to various warring Sunni militias. Such action, which is actually underway, is to be commended and encouraged.

Unfortunately, Iran and Qatar continue unabated in respectively supporting warring Shia and Sunni Moslems all around the region. Their action is not condoned, and the leaders of both countries need to reconsider their attitudes if there is to be any hope for ending conflicts in the ME.

Religious leaders could also play a constructive role by promoting tolerance as Al Azhar continues to do, instead of inciting trouble as many MB and Shia religious leaders indulged in doing. Religious leaders in the affected countries are implored to emulate the Al Azhar model, and to abstain from emulating the MB; in the least, by denouncing violence and promoting peaceful coexistence with others.

Many of the main players, both political and religious, seem to espouse the attitude of having 'all or nothing'; the notion of plurality and coexistence seems to escape most of them. Many leaders seem to be seeking 'victory' over their opponents with the aim of having full control of future developments without opposition. For example, after assuming power in Egypt the MB acted systematically to prevent others from sharing power in the future. The Egyptians were smart enough to sense that, and to act to prevent an MB takeover of the country. After the second revolution the MB was invited to participate in political developments. Instead of obliging, they reverted to terrorism in an attempt to revive their dreams of hegemony. By opting this way they precluded themselves from future political participation. To all such imprudent leaders, the Tunisian experiment is recommended as a worthy example to be appreciated and emulated.

After initiating the Arab Spring, MB sympathetic entities assumed control in Tunisia. However, the Egyptian second revolution inspired the Tunisians to challenge the influence of the Islamist parties that came to power after deposing Bin Ali. Having witnessed what transpired in Egypt, the Tunisians moved to reinstate secularism.

The Tunisian people are being praised internationally for having achieved this transition in a civilized way, and for having crafted and adopted a commendable secular constitution. Notably, the leaders of the main Islamist Party Al Nahdah, unlike MB leaders, were wise enough to read public sentiments and to act in a responsible manner that ensured their presence in the political scene. Recent elections led to secular parties gaining a majority of seats in the Parliament, and presidential elections led to the election of a secularist President. Islamist parties though still hold a large number of parliamentary seats and continue to be active in the political arena. Although the country continues to suffer from terrorist acts by Islamist extremists, Tunisia is steadily moving towards a stable democracy.

The Tunisians and the Egyptians have already set up remarkable examples to learn from and perhaps emulate. The Tunisians led the revolt against despotic rulers, and the Egyptians led the way to contain radical Islamism. Generally, from my perspective, the more countries that emulate Egypt's drive towards secularity while pursuing their quest as the Tunisian did, the better will be the prospects for improving conditions in the Middle East region.

Last but not least, local Arab and Moslem populations need to be alert and discriminating in their attitudes towards the rhetoric of many of their political and religious leaders. Thankfully, the Arab Spring seems to have ushered an era where such general attitudes are beginning to prevail.

Update

As I prepared to go to print in mid April, 2015, the Arab League took a momentous decision to form a strike force to address the current crisis in the ME. Saudi Arabia and the UAE, actually started military action in Yemen by bombarding military targets there, and Egypt sent four navy ships towards the Red Sea shores of Yemen.

While I maintain my steadfast preference for negotiating solutions to political issues, I must point out that conditions in Yemen were spiraling in dangerous directions. The Yemeni Shia Houthis supported by Iran were on the verge of taking complete control of Yemen. The Saudis could not tolerate the presence of a pro Iranian government on their Southern borders. Also, the Egyptians who are investing billions to attract increased shipping traffic through the Suez Canal, could not tolerate Iranian control of shipping traffic exiting the Red Sea within striking range of an Iranian controlled Yemen. Furthermore, Yemen's Foreign Minister called for the allied Arab countries to urgently send troops on the ground to fight the Houthies and their Iranian 'advisors'.

Iran might have underestimated the potential reaction of Arab countries to its blatant activities in Yemen. Alternatively, it is perhaps luring the Arabs into a military land engagement in Yemen? Western Powers, including the USA approve of Arab action, and are supporting UN resolutions to legitimize it. The ultimate consequences of these ominous developments are difficult to foresee at the moment; they could conceivably lead to outright civil war in Yemen.

The moral though is that Western Powers are pulling away from direct military involvement in the ME, and that the Arabs are finally shedding foreign influence, and attending to sorting out their own affairs; in my view, a positive development all around.

Chapter 5

ZIONISM AND ISLAMISM AND THE SEPARATION OF STATE AND RELIGION

To begin with, I wish to dispose of the notion that Judaism and Islam per se lie at roots of problems.

Many political figures seeking favors from the Jewish community both here in the USA and elsewhere have expressed the facetious argument that Islam is an inherently 'bad' religion, because it promotes unacceptable courses of action to its followers. I certainly beg to differ. For example, prescribing the barbaric act of stoning to death is indicated as an appropriate method of punishment for certain similar offenses both in Judaism and in Islam. Does this make Judaism, and Islam, inherently 'bad' religions!? None of the aforementioned kind of politicians would agree to that! At any rate, neither Judaism nor Islam is per se the 'cause' of problems in the region.

Judaism, Christianity, and Islam have much in common: worship the one and only 'God', and do not lie, steal, or kill. However, Judaism and Islam promote 'an eye for an eye', while Christianity promotes 'turning the other cheek'. There are many other differences between monotheist religions including the prescribed frequency and time of prayer, and sundry dictates regarding social and individual behavior; for example: marry once and stay married until death separates you from your spouse, vs. you can marry up to four women and divorce anyone of them at will. Now, 'God Almighty' cannot be construed as being inconsistent, or thought of as having 'changed his position' regarding his dictates to humanity. Therefore, one tries to explain the discrepancies among monotheist religions.

One way of explanation is that God being aware of all conditions over time conceived dictates that were most effective in addressing contemporary ills in the societies of his respective prophets. This explanation though raises the issue that conditions have changed considerably over the millennia. Thus, in the lack of updated dictates, what are we supposed to do now vis-à-vis the existing contradictions among the three monotheist religions?

One way out of this dilemma is to claim that only one of the three monotheist religions is valid while the other two are not. The 'official' leaders of the three monotheist religions however unanimously reject this approach; thankfully, since otherwise we would be in real trouble. Another explanation is that the prophets Moses, Christ, and Mohammed who were no doubt social reformers of the first order, may have conceived some dictates on their own to address contemporary ills that turned out to be inconsistent in the long term. Reporting of the contradictory aspects of the dictates of the three monotheist religions as being prescribed by God, or by the prophets themselves for that matter, could be attributed to the prophets' followers, and/or to human error in repeated word of mouth transmission and copying of scriptures over the centuries.

The reader may choose any explanation s/he sees fit and proper to explain the discrepancies among monotheist religions. The point I wish to stress though is to warn against literal and biased interpretations of scriptures, including the Torah, the Bible, and the Quran, as well as reported commands and directives attributed to the prophets.

Historically, biased interpretation of scriptures led many to believe that the sun rotates around the earth; those who disagreed were burned to the stake. Many in the USA today, in spite of overwhelming scientific evidence still believe that the universe was created in seven days 10,000 years ago; they recently built a museum depicting children playing in the presence of dinosaurs.

In the Middle Ages Christianity was the religion of most European Feudal States. The wars and destruction that ensued at the time are historically well documented. The Europeans learned their lesson from history and avoided reference to Christianity in the EU Constitution.

Monotheist religions promote ethical behavior, and have contributed to the evolution of civil society. However, civil society has evolved beyond the archaic circumstances that prevailed at the time of their inception.

Instead of promising hell or heaven in an afterlife in the way of punishment and reward, we have laws that stipulate punishments and rewards in response to people's 'bad' and 'good' behavior here on earth. We can now rely on contemporary civic structures that govern social interactions, and need not rely on outdated and often contradictory prescriptions to maintain social peace and order.

Secular civic structures and laws evolved over the centuries to embody optimum measures, and minimum restrictions on individual and social behavior that ensure social stability. This is the clear advantage of secularity. The involvement of religion in state affairs tends to introduce additional archaic measures and restrictions that are neither needed nor acceptable to all. Thus, I am for creating a wall of separation between religion and state, and for keeping religious considerations as far away as possible from interfering with both civil and civic affairs.

By promoting a 'Jewish Nation State', Zionism brought about detrimental conditions in the ME that have lasted for decades. Had the MB remained in power, they would have imposed views that would have negatively impacted the lives of emancipated Sunni Moslems, the minorities of Shia Moslems and Copts, and Egyptian secular liberals in ways comparable to those that many Iranians have endured for decades since the institution of Iranian theocratic rule. ISIS's action reflects the extreme end of the spectrum of religious radicalism disregarding other peoples' dignity and lives. I dare not contemplate the conditions that might prevail if they would be allowed to have an 'Islamic Caliphate of their own'!

Zionism, the Moslem Brotherhood, Hamas, Hezbollah, Al-Qaida, ISIS, and other ideologies and entities involved in the ME crisis all display various degrees of religious prejudice. I do not mean that they are comparable, or equally culpable in their respective contributions to negative developments in the region. Rather, they all display a common denominator of religious prejudice and disregard for the rights and welfare of others which range from imposing mere inconvenient conditions such as women having to wear a hejab even if they do not wish to do so, to occupation and humiliation, and to outright slaughter of those who do not toe the line. Therefore, I do not condone the involvement of such ideologies and entities in the state affairs of any country in the region, or anywhere else in the world for that matter.

Emancipation from archaic attitudes could be approached through appropriate religious education that emphasizes the essence of all religions, instead of emphasizing and promoting the differences between various religions and sects, which often reflect bias from the common spirit of all scriptures. Education in philosophy and science would also broaden the perspective of present and future generations of young people, and thus help in stemming the spread of religious extremism and its dangerous consequences.

TV programs in the US show young boys in Pakistani 'madrasas'- elementary schools- repeatedly shaking their heads as they are taught to recite the Quran. This is not much different from Sephardic Jews repeatedly shaking their heads as they pray in front of the Whaling Wall. It is sad to observe that religious persuasion is accidental to one's place of birth, and that religious leaders of different persuasions have devised powerful tactics to indoctrinate their followers in ways that are extremely difficult to undo. Accordingly, addressing the roots of religious bias, and emancipation from its grip, could take generations to achieve.

Addressing Islamism through education is now generally recognized locally and internationally as necessary in combating terrorism. For example, the governments of Saudi Arabia, the UAE, Kuwait, Bahrain, and Egypt are replacing radical imams with moderate ones, and mobilizing their local religious leaders to promote tolerance and true religious values in public speeches, in Friday sermons in mosques, and in teaching classes at schools. I am not aware of similar moves to address Zionism!

Addressing Islamism in many Moslem countries predicates addressing economic issues. The relatively poor have been traditionally prone to indoctrination by fanatic religious leaders. In addition, it is generally recognized that adverse economic conditions reflected in high percentages of poverty and unemployment are responsible for many upheavals in the region. The countries of the region are demographically 'young', with millions of unemployed young people yearning for some way to make a decent living. Therefore, one of the main priorities for action to diffuse tensions in the region would be to provide employment opportunities to millions of unemployed young people.

It is sad to observe that many ME countries have large communities of poor radical Moslems. The socioeconomic dynamics that led to this state of affairs are intricate and difficult to cover. They involve the low status of women in society, poor education, lack of industrial development, and sundry other factors. Accordingly, blame for negative socioeconomic conditions and their consequences could be partially attributed to the persistence of certain Islamist ideologies and to the adoption of archaic practices by some Islamist governments. Thus, addressing religion related issues in Moslem countries could have the added benefit of improving economic conditions.

Addressing the issues relating to Zionism, could certainly have wide ranging constructive ramifications!

As mentioned above, religious bias and radicalism result from deeply ingrained indoctrination, and thus it could take generations to emancipate large enough numbers of people from their radical religious attitudes to affect meaningful change. In the mean time therefore, people are urged to consider the essence of all religions: "Do unto others, what you would have others do unto you". Honest and serious consideration of this adage would certainly help in diffusing many kinds of global issues.

Also, large numbers of people around the globe will continue for some time to harbor rigid religious attitudes and attempt to impose their views on others. The debate over abortion in the USA is a prominent example of such attitudes. Those who continue to harbor such attitudes are advised to accept the notion of plurality and to adopt the adage 'live and let live'. They are free to adhere to the dictates of their beliefs, and should allow others the same privilege; within reason of course, since one cannot allow some of us to chop the heads of others because they believe that this is 'right' thing to do.

Epilogue

In summary, three main categories of issues have negatively impacted developments in the Middle East.

The first category relating to Israel is the most stubborn; it has persisted with scantly any change for over six decades. PM Netanyahu's attitude and his success in the recent elections in Israel confirm that, left to its own devices, Israel is not likely to change its posture without international pressure on Israeli rightwing politicians to modify their views. Accordingly, the international community is urged to take whatever measures it sees fit to convince Israel to change its unsustainable stance.

The second category relates to the negative influence of Western Imperialism which the US assumed after the demise of the British Empire. Western Powers, including the US acted adversely in the region for quite some time, but have favorably changed their approach in the ME since President Obama took office. The US and its allies need to continue their recent more positive attitudes. However, the US in particular, needs to change its attitude toward Egypt as suggested in chapter 3 and, above all, change its attitude toward Israel!

The third category regarding the action of local populations and their leaders will continue to affect future developments. Thus, local leaders such as those in Tunisia, Egypt, Saudi Arabia, and other GCC countries who have taken steps to address inherent problems in the region, need to continue their positive contribution. The late King Abdullah of Saudi Arabia is to be thanked for his prudent leadership in these respects. His successor, King Salman, is astutely following suit. Others such as Iran and Qatar need to recognize their reprehensible involvement in flaring the current crisis and to act as suggested in chapter 4.

The UN is the next most important entity affecting developments in the ME region. It has been doing what it could to address several 'crises' in the region and around the world. Thus the UN needs to continue its efforts. Unfortunately however, the UN's contributions are relatively limited and constrained; if it had the power to implement its resolutions we would not be where we are today!

Alas, the UN Charter gives the five permanent members of the Security Council, namely China, France, the Russian Federation, the United Kingdom, and the United States, the right to veto the decisions of the world community of nations at large. This has proven to constitute a major stumbling obstacle to the UN in carrying out its mission. In my book "Planning for Survival" (2008), I argue for the urgent need to revamp the UN Charter.

The Arab Spring ushered a new era in the Middle East whereby the people of the region have begun to forcefully express their views, instead of succumbing to despotic rule. Islamist entities such as the Sunni Moslem Brotherhood and the Shia Iranian leadership attempted, and continue to attempt to take advantage of the moment to spread theocratic rule. Their quest could be attributed to sincere religious beliefs. However, I am convinced that their efforts, especially in the case of Iran, relate essentially to their desire to expand their influence in the region for political advantage.

Large numbers of the people in the ME aspire to establishing some form of democracy that allows them freedom of speech and provide a vehicle by which they would be empowered to affect political considerations in their respective countries; the young Egyptians who were instrumental in initiating the first and second revolutions certainly aimed for that. Now, establishing the rule of Sharia Law cannot be expected to pave the way for such aspirations; religious laws tend to be 'set in stone' and thus, are not amenable to open democratic discussion and possible modification.

In my book "For the People by the People" (2011) I clearly express my faith in democratic principles. However, I point out the pitfalls inherent in their application in practice, by citing negative conditions that have prevailed in the USA for many years now; 'the practice of democracy' in Israel also illustrates my point. In this book, I hope that I have argued convincingly for the advantages of separating religion from state affairs. The views expressed in the two books lead me to take the following considered position regarding recent developments in the ME.

Ideally, one aspires for a 'secular democracy' which embraces democratic principles while, at the same time, keeping a wall separating religion from state affairs. The Tunisian experience appears to be close to achieving such an ideal; thus, it earned international recognition and admiration. On the other hand, the Egyptian experiment while keeping religious considerations at bay, is still struggling with full implementation of democratic principles; mainly due to the intransigence of militant Islamists. This predicament does not worry me as much as it does many progressive thinkers whose views I respect. From my perspective, my concerns over the spread of Islamism which I highlighted, readily trump my concerns over the judicious pursuit of democratic principles, which is anyway rather problematic under the prevailing circumstances in the region.

The enduring problems in the Middle East continue to have international repercussions, and constitute one of the main issues that deserve the attention and action of the international community. In addition to human suffering and devastation, and the expenditure of enormous resources towards reconstruction and building up military forces in the region, they led to the institution of sundry undesirable and costly measures in the West to counter the threat from terrorist acts by radical Islamists.

As I argued in "Planning for Survival", the highest priority for action by the international community lies in addressing numerous ominous threats to human survival. Strategically, in a global context, ME problems by comparison appear to be rather mundane and petty. However, their persistence is wasting tremendous resources, and is distracting our attention from the more important strategic issues affecting the survival of the human race.

Printed in the United States
by Baker & Taylor Publisher Services